More Winning Recipes
from our
Members and Leaders

Over 60 recipes low in points

SIMON & SCHUSTER
A VIACOM COMPANY

Edited by Becky Johnson

First published in Great Britain by Simon & Schuster UK Ltd, 2002.
A Viacom Company.

Copyright © 2002, Weight Watchers International, Inc.

Simon & Schuster UK Ltd.
Africa House
64–78 Kingsway
London WC2B 6AH

Weight Watchers and *Pure Points* are Trademarks
of Weight Watchers International, Inc. and used under its
control by Weight Watchers (UK) Ltd.

Photography and styling: Steve Baxter
Food preparation: Sara Buenfeld
Design: Jane Humphrey
Typesetting: Stylize Digital Artwork
Printed and bound in China

Weight Watchers Publications Manager: Corrina Griffin
Weight Watchers Publications Executive: Lucy Davidson
Weight Watchers Competition Judges: Sue Beveridge,
Sue Ashworth, Celia Whiston

A CIP catalogue record for this book is available
from the British Library

ISBN 0 743 23090 6

Pictured on the front cover: (Clockwise) Garlic, Herb and Smoked Ham Tagliatelle (page 23);
Mediterranean Vegetables with Camembert (page 7); Fish Pie with Potato Topping (page 32);
Strawberry Cheesecake (page 54).
Pictured on the back cover: Pineapple and Passion-Fruit Squares (page 56)
Pictured on the title page: Hot Bacon and Plum Salad (page 19)

Raw Eggs: Only the freshest eggs should be used. Pregnant women, the elderly and children
should avoid recipes with eggs which are raw or not fully cooked.

V denotes a vegetarian recipe and assumes vegetarian cheese and
free-range eggs are used. Virtually fat-free fromage frais and
low-fat crème fraîche may contain traces of gelatine so they are
not always vegetarian: please check the labels.

Vg denotes a vegan dish.

contents

Thank you to everyone who entered recipes in our competition. There were so many wonderful creations – it made the judging a real challenge this year! Congratulations to all our winners, and especially to the chapter winners.

I've really enjoyed working on Weight Watchers Winning Recipes from our Members and Leaders. Considering how many Weight Watchers Members love food and, as a result, are passionate home cooks, it is no surprise that these recipes are of a very high standard. It seems that Weight Watchers Members, far from being daunted by the challenge to develop low-fat, low-calorie food, are instead inspired not only to adapt their own family favourites, but also to innovate and create original and delicious dishes.

more of your winning recipes

The ingredients and flavours used here have been drawn from cuisines all over the world. Ideas and tastes have been picked up from relatives abroad, or foods tried on holidays like Thai-Style Carrot and Coriander Soup, (page 13), Moroccan Stuffed Plaice (page 31) and Quorn and Chick-Pea Tikka (page 42). There is also the more traditional, home-grown fare cooked in new and exciting ways like Pork with Creamy Mushroom and Peppercorn Sauce (page 30), Sausage Casserole with Leek and Onion Mash (page 41) and Fresh Strawberry Ice Cream (page 53).

It's obvious that Members really enjoy the Weight Watchers 'no food is forbidden' concept since you'll find it everywhere in this book. You'll also see that traditionally banned foods are used very cleverly in the recipes! Try the sumptuous Zuccotto (page 48), Strawberry Cheesecake (page 54) and Thai Coconut Cod with Fruited Pilau Rice (page 29). Recipes that might normally be considered mundane are given lots of wonderful creative twists which make them absolutely delicious: there's Fish Pie with Potato Topping (page 32) and Veggie Cobbler (page 39), which uses a traditionally sweet recipe to make a homely, satisfying stew.

All the recipes are refreshingly easy to make and fuss-free. They often only take a few minutes. Best of all, they are created by fellow Weight Watchers and the emphasis is on full flavours and satisfaction with low, low point values – some have no points at all like the fabulous Zero-Point Chilli Soup (page 11)!

Special thanks must go to the sponsors of the competition, bamix. Made in Switzerland, bamix is a truly unique and powerful Hand Held Food Processor. It has been an indispensable aid in the kitchen for nearly 50 years as is proved by its daily use in over ten million households and catering establishments worldwide. It whips, blends, beats, aerates and chops; bamix is also capable of turning ordinary 'skimmed milk to a thick whipped cream consistency'. To obtain one, contact Proven Products Limited, Unit 3, Ellesmere Business Park, Haydn Road, Sherwood, Nottingham NG5 1DX; tel: 0115 960 8646; fax: 0115 969 3139; email: Sales@bamix-ppl.co.uk; www.bamixuk.com.

Mediterranean Vegetables with Camembert: This colourful salad with a delicious melted cheese topping is only 3 points per serving.

soups & starters

Soups are invaluable to our Members, especially throughout the autumn and winter months when we all crave something warming and satisfying. These soups will chase away any winter blues, and fill up empty tummies at the cost of very few points – and in some cases none at all. There are also some wonderful ideas for dips (great for party nibbles!), barbecues, packed lunches and picnics. So thank you to all the entrants for such wonderfully inspiring recipes to help get us through those hungry days.

MEDITERRANEAN VEGETABLES WITH CAMEMBERT

POINTS	
per recipe: 6	per serving: 3

ⓥ Serves 2

Preparation time: 10 minutes
Cooking time: 25 minutes
Calories per serving: 160
Freezing: not recommended

Mrs Kerry Hall is a Member from Irthlingborough in Northants. She is 36 and married with four children. She has two cooking jobs, one in a residential care home and one in an Italian bistro. She finds the points system works so well for her that after only two weeks with Weight Watchers, she proudly received her Silver Seven.

½ yellow pepper, chopped
½ red pepper, chopped
½ medium aubergine, chopped
1 medium courgette, chopped
low-fat cooking spray
75 g (2³/₄ oz) Camembert cheese, sliced thinly
a generous pinch of paprika
salt and freshly ground black pepper
rocket or other salad leaves, to serve

1 Preheat the oven to Gas Mark 4/ 180°C/fan oven 160°C and place all the vegetables in an ovenproof dish. Season and spray them with the cooking spray. Toss together and spray again.
2 Bake the vegetables in the oven for 15 minutes. Now lay the Camembert slices on top and sprinkle with paprika. Bake for a further 10 minutes until the Camembert is melted and the vegetables are golden.
3 Serve immediately on a bed of rocket or other salad leaves.

TOP TIP This dish can be served cold, by baking the vegetables without the cheese. You can keep them in the refrigerator for up to three days.

VARIATIONS Vary the vegetables with whatever zero-point ones are available, and try sprinkling them with fresh herbs like basil or rosemary.

You can also make this dish using Mozzarella Light instead of the Camembert. The points will be reduced to 2½ per serving.

WICKEDLY RED-HOT TOMATO SOUP

POINTS	
per recipe: 1/2	per serving: 0

(V) (Vg) *Serves 6*
Preparation time: 5 minutes
Cooking time: 20 minutes
Calories per serving: 35
Freezing: recommended

Jackie Coxhead is a Gold Member from Somercotes in Derbyshire. She made this recipe when she had some leftover tomato juice and since she grows her own chillies, she thought she'd combine the two. Her husband commented that it was "wicked" – hence the name, but with zero points per portion it's not just wicked it's fantastic!

low-fat cooking spray
1 large onion, chopped
2 garlic cloves, crushed
300 ml (1/2 pint) vegetable stock
1–2 fresh red chillies (to suit your own taste), de-seeded and chopped finely
1 litre (1 3/4 pints) tomato juice
1 teaspoon sugar
salt and freshly ground black pepper

1 Spray a large saucepan with the cooking spray, and fry the onion and garlic for 5 minutes, until softened – adding a little water if they begin to stick.
2 Add the stock, chillies, tomato juice and sugar, and bring to the boil. Lower the heat and simmer for about 10 minutes.
3 Liquidise the soup in a food processor or liquidiser. Season to taste and then serve.

CREAMY, SPICY CARROT DIP

POINTS	
per recipe: 6	per serving: 1 1/2

(V) *if using vegetarian cheese*
Serves 4
Preparation time: 15 minutes
Calories per serving: 100
Freezing: not recommended

Susanne Houghton is a Leader from Glemsford in Suffolk whose passion is cooking. The idea for this recipe came from a friend, but she has added a few extras and made it her own. Susanne and her husband enjoy it as a starter in the summer instead of soup, as it is filling, healthy and tasty.

200 g (7 oz) low-fat soft cheese
2 tablespoons low-fat plain yogurt
2 tablespoons tomato ketchup
2 medium carrots, grated finely
1/2 teaspoon sweet chilli sauce

TO SERVE

zero-point vegetable crudités (e.g. whole mange-tout peas or sugar snap peas; red, orange or yellow pepper, sliced into strips; cauliflower or broccoli cut into bite-size florets; spring onions, sliced lengthways; carrots or cucumber, cut into long slices)

1 Mix together all the dip ingredients and spoon into a serving dish. Place in the centre of a large plate of vegetable crudités and serve.

VARIATIONS For a creamier dip, use half-fat crème fraîche rather than yogurt. The points will be 2 per serving.
   Try using Worcestershire or Tabasco sauce instead of the sweet chilli sauce. The points will remain the same.

CHUNKY CHICKEN CHOWDER

POINTS	
per recipe: 7	per serving: 3 1/2

Serves 2
Preparation time: 15 minutes
Cooking time: 40 minutes
Calories per serving: 330
Freezing: recommended

Caroline Gibbs, a Member from Gorleston in Great Yarmouth, is a busy mum of three with a part-time job. This recipe is ideal, as she cooks it on her days off, and then enjoys it over the two days she works when she doesn't have time to prepare meals. Caroline says this soup is also a good way to get fussy-eaters to enjoy vegetables as her 7 year-old daughter loves it too!

1 medium skinless chicken breast (165 g/5 3/4 oz), trimmed of any fat and diced
425 ml (3/4 pint) chicken or vegetable stock
2 medium carrots, grated
2 medium leeks, sliced
1/2 medium swede, diced
2 tablespoons dried yellow lentils, rinsed
300 ml (1/2 pint) semi-skimmed milk
2 tablespoons fresh, frozen or canned sweetcorn
salt and freshly ground black pepper

1 Place all the ingredients except the milk and sweetcorn in a large saucepan and bring to the boil.
2 Turn down the heat and simmer for 25–30 minutes, and then add the milk and sweetcorn. Season, warm through for a further 10 minutes on a gentle heat before serving.

Chunky Chicken Chowder: Enjoy a warming and satisfying bowl for only 3½ points.

FRENCH BROCCOLI & BUTTER BEAN SOUP

V Vg Serves 2

Preparation time: 20 minutes
Cooking time: 15 minutes
Calories per serving: 205
Freezing: recommended

Jo Dunnachie is an enthusiastic Leader from the most northern Weight Watchers class in the UK, in Inverness-shire. She lost 108 pounds on the Weight Watchers programme before becoming a Leader, and now takes eight Meetings a week. She is married with a 10 year-old daughter and is passionate about both cooking and France – hence this soup is a delightful combination of the two!

300 g (10½ oz) broccoli, broken into florets
1 medium onion, chopped
3 garlic cloves, crushed
1 tablespoon dried herbes de Provence
850 ml (1½ pints) vegetable stock
200 g can of butter beans, rinsed and drained
salt and freshly ground black pepper
2 × 5 cm (2-inch) slices of French bread, to serve

1 Place the broccoli, onion, garlic, herbs, seasoning and stock in a saucepan and bring to the boil. Turn down the heat and simmer for 15 minutes, until the broccoli is tender.
2 Blend the soup in a liquidiser or food processor with the butter beans, and then return it to the pan. Warm the soup through, check the seasoning, and serve each bowlful with a slice of French bread.

VARIATIONS If you are not keen on broccoli, you can make this soup with mushrooms.

For a dinner party, try making a creamy version by adding 1 tablespoon of half-fat crème fraîche to each bowl. This would bring the points up to 3 per serving.

Chip 'n' Dip: A fantastic snack.

CHIP 'N' DIP

V Vg Serves 4

Preparation time: 15 minutes
Cooking time: 1 hour
Calories per serving: 205
Freezing: recommended (for the dip)

Mrs Deborah Jeffreys is a Member from Blaina in Gwent. She created this as an alternative to the fat-laden crinkle-cut chips, and cream or mayonnaise-based dips often served at parties and barbecues. Deborah likes to adapt recipes rather than do without, and, having lost 24 pounds so far, she has proved that this philosophy works.

FOR THE DIP
2 × 400 g cans of plum tomatoes
2 large fresh red chillies, de-seeded
1 large red onion, chopped coarsely
2 tablespoons artificial sweetener (or to taste)
a small bunch of fresh basil, or 2 pinches dried mixed herbs
salt and freshly ground black pepper

FOR THE CHIPS
2 × 400 g (14 oz) large baking potatoes, peeled
low-fat cooking spray
a pinch of paprika
salt and freshly ground black pepper

1 Drain the tomatoes of liquid and place them in a blender. Add all the other dip ingredients and process until everything is chopped finely.
2 Pour the dip into a large saucepan and bring to the boil. Turn down the heat and leave to simmer gently for 45 minutes–1 hour, until it is reduced down and thickened. Check the seasoning.
3 Meanwhile preheat the oven to Gas Mark 6/200°C/fan oven 180°C. Cut the potatoes into 3 mm (⅛-inch) thin slices and place them on a large baking tray. Season the slices with paprika and salt and pepper. Spray with the low-fat cooking spray and toss the potatoes to coat them – then spray again.
4 Roast the potatoes in a single layer in the oven for 20 minutes, turning once or twice, until golden and crispy. Serve the 'chips' with the dip.

TOP TIP Both the chips and the dip can be served hot or cold.

MUSHROOM PÂTÉ

POINTS

per recipe: 16   per serving: 1½

Ⓥ *if using a free-range egg*
Serves 12
Preparation time: 15 minutes
Cooking time: 1¼ hours
Calories per serving: 90
Freezing: not recommended

Ann Pattinson is a Member from Jesmond in Newcastle-Upon-Tyne. She is a retired paediatric theatre sister whose hobbies include charity work, dressmaking and rescuing abandoned animals. Ann has yet to meet anyone who doesn't like her version of this pâté. It's versatile enough to be served hot or cold; as a starter or a snack.

1 medium egg
1 teaspoon marmite
3 garlic cloves, chopped
2 medium onions, chopped
500 g (1 lb 2 oz) mushrooms, chopped
100 g (3½ oz) fresh white breadcrumbs
100 g (3½ oz) nut pieces, chopped (choose from walnuts, hazelnuts or cashew nuts)
a small bunch of fresh parsley, thyme, oregano or coriander, chopped
salt and freshly ground black pepper

1 Preheat the oven to Gas Mark 4/ 180°C/fan oven 160°C. Line a 20 cm (8-inch) round and at least 6 cm (2½-inch) deep cake tin or ovenproof dish with non-stick baking parchment.

2 Beat the egg and the marmite together in a large bowl, until the marmite dissolves. Add all the other ingredients. Toss everything together well and then spoon into the tin.

3 Bake for 1¼ hours and then leave to cool in the dish, or serve hot.

TOP TIPS The pâté will keep in the refrigerator for up to three days.

It is best served from the baking dish as it sometimes will not turn out in one piece.

ZERO-POINT CHILLI SOUP

POINTS

per recipe: 0   per serving: 0

Ⓥ Ⓥⓖ *Serves 4*
Preparation time: 15 minutes
Cooking time: 20 minutes
Calories per serving: 55
Freezing: not recommended

Mrs Heather McLaren is a Gold Member from Winchester. She first joined Weight Watchers in February 1977 and lost 32 pounds to reach Goal. She managed to stay reasonably within her Goal for three years before trips abroad and hotel stays made the weight creep back on. She returned to Weight Watchers in January 2001 and has lost 16 pounds to date. She loves soups and with all those trips abroad, to the Far East especially, she has acquired an addiction to spicy food. Serve each portion of this soup with 1 teaspoon half-fat crème fraîche, adding the extra points.

1–2 fresh green chillies, de-seeded and chopped finely
150 g (5½ oz) green beans, each chopped into three
150 g (5½ oz) broccoli, broken into florets
150 g (5½ oz) dark green cabbage leaves, shredded
1 medium green pepper, chopped
1 medium onion, chopped
2 garlic cloves, chopped
850 ml (1½ pints) vegetable stock
salt and freshly ground black pepper
a few chopped chives, to garnish (optional)

1 Place all the ingredients in a large saucepan and bring to the boil. Turn down the heat and simmer for 15–20 minutes, until the vegetables are tender.

2 Liquidise the soup in a food processor or liquidiser. Check the seasoning and serve. Garnish with chives, if desired.

Zero-Point Chilli Soup: No points at all!

TOP TIP Instead of throwing away the stalks when cooking broccoli in other recipes, save and use them to make this soup.

On a hot day this soup can be eaten cold as a kind of green gazpacho.

VARIATION The outside leaves of a cauliflower make a good substitute for cabbage leaves.

**Thai-style Carrot
and Coriander
Soup: Only 1½
points for each
delicious serving.**

THAI-STYLE CARROT AND CORIANDER SOUP

POINTS	
per recipe: 6	per serving: 1½

(V) Serves 4

Preparation time: 20 minutes
Cooking time: 30 minutes
Calories per serving: 135
Freezing: recommended

Mrs C Wilson, a Gold Member from North Shields in Tyne and Wear, based this recipe on the vegetable soup recipes in the Weight Watchers magazines and cookbooks, but gave it her own unique twist. She particularly enjoys Thai flavourings, so she made sure she included them. She has 10 year-old twin boys and in her spare time, as well as cooking, she enjoys reading and surfing the Internet.

1 litre (1³/₄ pints) vegetable stock
1 large onion, chopped
750 g (1lb 10 oz) carrots, chopped
1 fresh red chilli, de-seeded and chopped
juice and zest of 1 lemon
2 garlic cloves, peeled
a bunch of fresh coriander, chopped
25 g (1 oz) creamed coconut
salt and freshly ground black pepper

TO GARNISH
fresh coriander leaves
fresh red or green chilli, chopped finely, or some dried chilli flakes (optional)

1 Place all the ingredients except the coconut and garnish in a large saucepan. Bring to the boil and then turn down the heat. Simmer for 25 minutes, until the vegetables are soft.
2 Add the creamed coconut. When the coconut has melted, liquidise the soup in a food processor or liquidiser until smooth. Taste and season. Serve garnished with fresh coriander and some finely chopped fresh chilli or dried chilli flakes if using.

VARIATION Omit the coconut for a zero-point soup or serve with 1 tablespoon of low-fat plain yogurt, but add the extra points.

PRAWN SURPRISE

POINTS	
per recipe: 5½	per serving: 1½

Serves 4

Preparation time: 10 minutes
Calories per serving: 85
Freezing: not recommended

Vanda Nowak is a Leader from Locksheath in Southampton. She has been a Leader for two years now and lost 20 pounds to reach her Goal. This recipe is one of her favourites for entertaining; she serves it in individual long-stemmed glasses.

125 g (4¹/₂ oz) prawns, cooked and peeled
400 g (14 oz) honeydew melon (approximately half a melon), cut into bite-sized pieces
1 or 2 celery sticks, sliced thinly
2 tablespoons low-fat mayonnaise
1 teaspoon curry powder
salt and freshly ground black pepper

TO SERVE
a few handfuls of salad leaves
1 lemon, cut into 4 wedges
a pinch of paprika

1 In a large bowl, toss together the prawns, melon, celery, mayonnaise, curry powder and seasoning.
2 Place some salad leaves in the base of four serving dishes, and then pile the prawn and melon mixture on top.
3 Serve each surprise with a wedge of lemon and a pinch of paprika to garnish.

VARIATION A red dessert apple cubed and added in step 1 makes a delicious addition to the dish. The points will remain the same.

Prawn Surprise: The classic starter for fewer points.

light meals
& salads

There's certainly nothing light or understated about the flavours in this chapter! The entries for these light meals greatly impressed the judges – the creativity and interesting combinations of tastes are truly inspiring. From the absolutely delicious Hot Bacon and Plum Salad (page 19) to the more-ish Courgette Fritters (page 21), there's something to suit everyone who just wants a light bite. They're quick and easy too, so get cooking!

ROAST VEGETABLE QUICHE

POINTS

per recipe: 9   per serving: 2½

Ⓥ if using a free-range egg

Serves 4
Preparation time: 15 minutes
Cooking time: 40–45 minutes
Calories per serving: 215
Freezing: recommended

Valerie Kitching is a Gold Member from Kendal in Cumbria. She loves to cook and enjoys trying out new flavours. She finds the Weight Watchers cookbooks helpful and really encouraging. She developed this recipe for her sister who also loves food but cannot eat pastry. As well as cooking, she finds time for swimming, gardening, quilting and, now that they are both retired, she and her husband often go motoring.

1 medium green, 1 medium red and 1 medium yellow pepper, de-seeded and sliced

1 medium red onion, sliced into 8

4 shallots, quartered

4 medium carrots, sliced

low-fat cooking spray

450 g (1 lb) potatoes, cut into chunks

1 tablespoon horseradish sauce

1 large egg

150 ml (¼ pint) skimmed milk

2 tablespoons half-fat Cheddar cheese, grated

salt and freshly ground black pepper

1 Preheat the oven to Gas Mark 7/ 220°C/fan oven 200°C. Place all the vegetables apart from the potatoes in a roasting tray. Season and spray them with the cooking spray. Toss together and spray again. Roast the vegetables for 20 minutes, until soft and golden.

2 Meanwhile, boil the potatoes in lightly salted water. Drain and mash them with the horseradish sauce and seasoning.

3 Line a 20 cm (8-inch) loose-bottomed cake tin with non-stick baking parchment. Spoon in the mash and press down to form a base. Bake in the oven for 10 minutes, until the potato has formed a crust.

4 Pile the roasted vegetables on top of the potato base. In a jug beat together the egg and milk with some seasoning. Pour the egg mixture over the vegetables, and then sprinkle over the grated cheese. Return to the oven for a further 10–15 minutes, until the top is set and golden. Serve hot or cold.

Roast Vegetable Quiche: Each tasty slice has only 2½ points.

Cool Herby Chicken: A fabulous light meal with fresh, zingy flavours.

COOL HERBY CHICKEN

POINTS

per recipe: 14   per serving: 2½

ⓥ *if following variation*

Serves 6

Preparation time: 10–15 minutes

Calories per serving: 125

Freezing: not recommended

Tracey Bryan, a Gold Member from Lytham in Lancashire, initially joined Weight Watchers to lose weight for her wedding. She succeeded and has maintained her ideal weight for over a year now. The inspiration for this recipe is rather romantic because the idea came from a meal she was served in a Greek taverna on the island of Crete, where she first met her husband.

150 ml (5 fl oz) 0% fat Greek yogurt
150 ml (5 fl oz) half-fat crème fraîche
a small bunch of fresh coriander, chopped
a small bunch of fresh parsley, chopped
a small bunch of fresh mint, chopped
6 spring onions, sliced finely
2 × 125 g (4½ oz) cooked medium skinless chicken breasts, cut into bite-sized pieces
1½ teaspoons ground coriander
1½ teaspoons ground cumin
salt and freshly ground black pepper
a few sprigs of fresh coriander, mint and parsley, to garnish
crisp green salad leaves, to serve

1 Combine all the ingredients in a large bowl. Leave to stand for at least 5 minutes to allow time for the flavours to develop.

2 Spoon the mixture on to serving plates, garnish with sprigs of fresh herbs. Serve with a crisp green salad.

VARIATION Try using chopped cucumber instead of chicken for a delicious vegetarian alternative. The points will be reduced to 1½ per serving.

BREAKFAST OMELETTE

POINTS

per recipe: 2½   per serving: 2½

ⓥ *if using a free-range egg*

Serves 1

Preparation and cooking time: 15 minutes

Calories per serving: 135

Freezing: not recommended

Mrs Sue Chorley is a Member from Newport on the Isle of Wight. Because of her intolerance to milk, cereals and bread, she had difficulty finding a breakfast that would be both appetising and able to carry her through the morning. Then she remembered the sweet omelettes she had enjoyed years ago for brunch at the restaurant near to the further education college where she taught. This is her version of them.

100 g (3½ oz) fresh raspberries
1 large egg, separated
1 teaspoon artificial sweetener
low-fat cooking spray

1 Reserving a few raspberries for a garnish, roughly chop the rest.

2 Whisk the egg white until dry and fluffy, and then whisk the egg yolk into the egg white.

3 Stir the sweetener into the egg mixture, and then spray a small, non-stick frying pan with the cooking spray.

4 Heat the pan for a couple of minutes and then pour in the egg mixture. Spread it around evenly with a spatula and cook for 2 minutes or until the bottom is browned.

5 Flip the omelette and press it down with the spatula. Immediately pile the raspberries on top and cook for a further 2 minutes.

6 Fold the omelette in half and slide it out of the pan on to a plate. Garnish with the remaining fresh raspberries and eat immediately.

Mediterranean Salad: Lots of colour and lots to eat for only 4½ points per serving.

MEDITERRANEAN SALAD

POINTS

per recipe: 18½   per serving: 4½

Ⓥ *if following variation*

Serves 4

Preparation time: 20 minutes

Cooking time: 30 minutes

Calories per serving: 385

Freezing: not recommended

Susan Taylor is a Member who first joined Weight Watchers when she decided to take positive action about her weight. She joined Dawn Broughton's Meeting in Beeston, Leeds and lost 2 stone. Now, three years on, she lives in Bangkok where her husband works, but she returned to Dawn's group last May for a 'kickstart' to lose the weight that had begun to creep back on. She has now lost 8½ pounds and is motivated to continue on her own, although her husband has promised her a trip home soon for another dose of Dawn's enthusiasm! This recipe evolved within her Programme as it's filling, tasty, versatile and low in points.

1 medium red pepper, de-seeded and chopped

1 medium courgette, halved lengthways and sliced into 1 cm (½-inch) pieces

1 teaspoon dried oregano or mixed herbs

low-fat cooking spray

250 g (9 oz) dried pasta

2 × 125 g cans of tuna in brine, drained

mixed salad leaves

180 g bag of baby spinach

8 cherry tomatoes, quartered

20 black olives

1 small red onion, sliced finely

a small bunch of fresh basil

salt and freshly ground black pepper

FOR THE DRESSING

3 tablespoons balsamic vinegar

1 tablespoon olive oil

1 teaspoon French mustard

1 teaspoon clear honey

salt and freshly ground black pepper

1 Preheat the oven to Gas Mark 6/ 200°C/fan oven 180°C. Place the pepper and courgette in a large roasting tin or on a baking sheet. Sprinkle with the herbs and seasoning, and spray with the cooking spray.

2 Roast for 10 minutes and then toss the vegetables around. Cook for another 10 minutes until they are browned and beginning to soften. Leave to cool.

3 Meanwhile cook the pasta as instructed on the packet. Drain, rinse in cold water, drain again and place in a large bowl.

4 Add the tuna, salad leaves, spinach, tomatoes, olives, onion, basil and the roasted vegetables to the pasta. Just before serving place all the dressing ingredients in a screw-topped jar and shake. Pour the dressing over the salad and toss together.

TOP TIP This is a good salad to use up any leftover pasta.

VARIATIONS Try experimenting with different zero-point vegetables such as aubergine, canned artichoke hearts and fennel.

You can make this into a vegetarian dish by simply leaving out the tuna.

HOT BACON AND PLUM SALAD

POINTS

per recipe: 14½   per serving: 7½

Serves 2
Preparation and cooking time:
20 minutes
Calories per serving: 385
Freezing: not recommended

Bridgette Read is a Gold Member from Eastry in Kent. She reached her Goal weight by losing 2 stone 6 pounds in 14 months. She is married to a self-employed builder and they have three children. Bridgette works as a learning support assistant at a local primary school, and spends her spare time creating new recipes and cycling.

12 plums: 6 stoned and quartered,
the others left whole

2 medium rashers lean back bacon,
rind and fat removed

1 garlic clove, crushed

1 small fresh green chilli, de-seeded
and chopped finely

2 teaspoons olive oil

2 teaspoons balsamic vinegar

1 teaspoon soy sauce

1 teaspoon lime juice

a few crisp salad leaves

100 g (3½ oz) feta cheese, cubed

200 g (7 oz) mange-tout peas

salt and freshly ground black pepper

1 Cook the six whole plums in a saucepan with 4 tablespoons of water for about 10 minutes, until softened.

2 Meanwhile, grill the bacon and then cut into small pieces. Put the garlic, chilli, olive oil, balsamic vinegar, soy sauce, lime juice and seasoning in a small bowl and whisk together to make the dressing.

3 Push the cooked plums through a sieve. Mix this plum purée into the dressing, stirring well.

4 Arrange the salad leaves on two serving plates and then pile the feta cheese, mange-tout peas, quartered plums and the bacon on top. Pour over the dressing and serve.

TOP TIP This is a great salad to make when plums are in season and plentiful. If you have more plums than you need you can cook and sieve them, and then keep the purée frozen in ice cube trays.

Hot Bacon and Plum Salad: Scrumptious and so easy to make!

LOUISE'S SUPER ROLLS

POINTS

per recipe: 16   per serving: 2

Serves 8
Preparation time: 15 minutes
Cooking time: 15–20 minutes
Calories per serving: 120
Freezing: not recommended

Mrs Louise Iles is a Gold Member from Weston-Super-Mare in North Somerset. She has lost 5 stone on the Weight Watchers Programme and now she enjoys helping her Leader. She is also very grateful for the support that she has been given. This recipe was originally put together using leftovers in the fridge, but it was such a great success that she now makes it regularly. Serve with grilled tomatoes, mushrooms and peppers, or with a big, fresh zero-point salad.

8 slices of medium-cut white bread
low-fat cooking spray
3 shallots, chopped finely
75 g (2³/₄ oz) half-fat Cheddar cheese, grated
75 g (2³/₄ oz) wafer-thin turkey slices, cut into small pieces
¹/₂ teaspoon mustard powder
¹/₂ teaspoon dried mixed herbs
1 medium egg, beaten
salt and freshly ground black pepper

1 Preheat the oven to Gas Mark 5/ 190°C/fan oven 170°C and line a baking sheet with non-stick baking parchment.
2 Remove the crusts from the top and bottom of the bread – leaving the crusts on the sides. Roll each slice out slightly with a rolling pin.
3 Spray a frying pan with the cooking spray. Cook the shallots gently until softened, adding a little water if necessary to stop them sticking.
4 In a bowl mix together the shallots, cheese, turkey, mustard powder and herbs, then season to taste. Spoon this mixture equally between the eight slices of bread.
5 Roll up each slice and secure with a cocktail stick. Using a pastry brush, brush the underside of each roll with the beaten egg, and then place on the lined baking sheet. Finally brush all the tops of the rolls with the remaining egg. Bake in the oven for 5–10 minutes, until golden brown and crispy.

TOP TIP Soak the cocktail sticks in cold water before using them and they will be easier to remove when the rolls are cooked.

VARIATION Cut each roll into four after baking and serve as nibbles at a ¹/₂ point each.

QUICK AND EASY HUMMOUS

POINTS

per recipe: 6   per serving: 1¹/₂

Ⓥ Ⓥ̲ₑ *Serves 4*
Preparation time: 10 minutes
Calories per serving: 170
Freezing: not recommended

Felicity Stephens is a Member from Chichester in West Sussex who joined Weight Watchers when her baby was five months old. She wanted to lose the extra weight she had gained during pregnancy, but was worried to diet on her own in case she overdid things and her milk dried up. She has lost 19 pounds so far and has only 3¹/₂ more to go to Gold. Hummous is one of her favourite foods but the shop-bought variety can be very high in fat, so she came up with this version which is cheaper and more delicious too. Serve with pitta breads and salad remembering to add the extra points.

1 × 410 g can of chick-peas, rinsed and drained
2 tablespoons fat-free vinaigrette with garlic
1 teaspoon roasted sesame oil
salt and freshly ground black pepper

1 Process the chick-peas to fine crumbs in a food processor. Mix in the vinaigrette and sesame oil, and season to taste.

TOP TIP You can use any fat-free dressing and add a crushed garlic clove.

VARIATION Try adding lemon juice for an extra zing.

FRUIT AND RICE SALAD

POINTS

per recipe: 20½	per serving: 3½

Ⓥ Ⓥⓖ *Serves 6*
Preparation time: 10 minutes
Cooking time: 20–30 minutes
Calories per serving: 230
Freezing: not recommended

Mrs Eileen Iredale is a Member from Lytham St Annes in Lancashire. She has one daughter, two sons and five grandchildren. This recipe came from one of her relatives in Australia, and is often served at family gatherings.

125 g (4½ oz) long-grain rice
1 medium carrot, chopped
1 medium apple, cored and chopped
150 g can of pineapple chunks in juice, drained
1 medium red pepper, de-seeded and chopped
25 g (1 oz) raisins
25 g (1 oz) walnuts, chopped
25 g (1 oz) pine kernels, toasted
2 teaspoons curry powder
2 tablespoons lemon juice
1 tablespoon chutney
2 tablespoons olive or vegetable oil
salt and freshly ground black pepper

1 Cook the rice as directed on the packet, and then drain it. Refresh under cold water and place it in a large bowl.

2 Add all the other ingredients and toss together well before serving.

TOP TIP This salad can be made up to a day in advance and kept in the refrigerator.

VARIATION Vary the vegetables and fruit in this salad depending on what is available. Don't forget to vary the points according to what you add.

COURGETTE FRITTERS

POINTS

per recipe: 7½	per serving: 2

Ⓥ *if using free-range eggs*
Serves 4
Preparation and cooking time:
45 minutes
Calories per serving: 165
Freezing: not recommended

Mrs Andrea Altinbas, a Member from Maidstone in Kent, has a young daughter and son. In addition to her hobbies, she keeps busy by working at her daughter's school and getting involved in as many of the children's activities as possible. Andrea joined Weight Watchers in January 2001 and lost 19 pounds. We love the flavour of mint in these little fritters which Andrea serves with a tomato, red onion and cucumber salad dressed with lemon juice.

4 medium courgettes
1 small onion, peeled
2 medium eggs
a small bunch of fresh mint, chopped
a small bunch of fresh parsley, chopped
100 g (3½ oz) plain white flour
low-fat cooking spray
salt and freshly ground black pepper

1 Grate the courgettes and onion into a large bowl. Add the other ingredients apart from the flour and the cooking spray. Mix together well, and then stir in the flour to make a sticky mixture.

2 Heat a large non-stick frying pan and spray with the cooking spray. Drop 4 tablespoons of the courgette mixture in the pan to make about four small fritters – flatten them with the back of a spoon.

3 Fry the fritters for 4–5 minutes, until firm and golden and then flip them over with a fish slice. Fry again until cooked through. Transfer the fritters on to kitchen paper, and then spray the pan again to fry the next batch. The mixture should make about 12 fritters. Allow three fritters per person.

Courgette Fritters: Get creative with courgettes.

Garlic, Herb and Smoked Ham Tagliatelle: A great after-work supper – it's ready in minutes and very satisfying.

GARLIC, HERB AND SMOKED HAM TAGLIATELLE

POINTS

per recipe: 11   per serving: 5½

Ⓥ *if following variation*

Serves 2

Preparation and cooking time:
20 minutes

Calories per serving: 430

Freezing: not recommended

Alison Pacey from Swinderby in Lincoln is a Gold Member. She works as a staff nurse in the Accident and Emergency department at her local hospital. As a result of working shifts, she needs recipes that not only fit into her Programme, but are quick and easy to prepare, and popular with her family too. She developed this recipe by experimenting with pasta, one of her favourite foods.

---

125 g (4½ oz) tagliatelle

2 garlic cloves, crushed

1 medium leek, chopped

250 g (9 oz) mushrooms, sliced

1 tablespoon dried mixed herbs

125 ml (4 fl oz) vegetable stock

125 g (4½ oz) low-fat soft cheese

125 g (4½ oz) wafer-thin smoked ham

2 tablespoons skimmed milk

salt and freshly ground black pepper

---

1 Cook the tagliatelle in plenty of lightly salted boiling water, according to the instructions on the packet.

2 Meanwhile place the garlic, leek, mushrooms and herbs in a large saucepan with the stock and bring to the boil. Turn down the heat and then simmer for 10 minutes, until the leeks are soft.

3 Add the cheese, ham, milk and seasoning to the vegetables and mix together.

4 Drain the pasta and add it to the sauce tossing everything together well. Serve immediately.

VARIATIONS For a vegetarian version just omit the ham and use vegetarian cheese.

Try substituting wine for the stock although this will add 1 point per serving.

For a sweeter flavour try using onions instead of the leek.

PINEAPPLE LUNCH

POINTS

per recipe: 9   per serving: 2½

Serves 4

Preparation time: 15 minutes

Calories per serving: 180

Freezing: recommended

Elizabeth Gray, a Member from Hebron in Morpeth, is married with three grown-up sons. She has her own horse, which she rides at least three times a week. She also plays tennis, enjoys gardening, goes to the gym, does upholstery classes, and is getting to grips with computing and the Internet.

---

1 ripe medium-sized pineapple

225 g (8 oz) prawns, cooked and peeled

120 g tub of low-fat plain yogurt

4 celery sticks, sliced thinly

20 cashew nuts

salt and freshly ground black pepper

---

1 Cut the pineapple into quarters lengthways. Remove the flesh and dice it, leaving the shells intact. Set them aside.

2 In a large bowl carefully mix together the pineapple flesh and all the remaining ingredients, and season well. Spoon the salad back into the shells and serve. If you like, chill before serving.

VARIATION Try low-fat mayonnaise instead of yogurt and experiment with different nuts – but don't forget to alter the points accordingly.

There is a fabulous selection of meat and fish dishes in this chapter, ranging from the exotic to the traditional. They're all written by fellow Weight Watchers who have found that these recipes work well for them. Tasty and filling, they will satisfy even the most ravenous appetite. The flavours in these recipes are full and bold, and show just how diverse the tastes of Weight Watchers Members are. When you are longing for something new – turn to these exciting main meals.

HONEY AND BLACK PEPPER BEEF

POINTS

per recipe: $13\frac{1}{2}$ per serving: $3\frac{1}{2}$

Serves 4
Preparation and cooking time:
25 minutes
Calories per serving: 210
Freezing: recommended

Mrs Carol Shrimpton, from Great Barr in Birmingham has been a Member for a year now, and has recently reached her Goal weight and become a Gold Member. She is a mum with two grown-up sons who tried this recipe while on holiday, and enjoyed it so much she decided to make it herself when she got back. She usually serves it with rice or noodles, and adds the points accordingly.

1 teaspoon sesame oil

3×125 g ($4\frac{1}{2}$ oz) lean beef steaks, sliced into thin strips

1 medium onion, sliced very finely

2 garlic cloves, crushed

300 g ($10\frac{1}{2}$ oz) mange-tout peas or sugar snap peas

2 tablespoons clear honey

2 tablespoons soy sauce

2 tablespoons oyster sauce

2 tablespoons crushed black peppercorns

1 Heat the oil in a wok or frying pan until very hot, and then add the meat. Stir-fry for 2 minutes until browned, and then tip out on to a plate lined with kitchen paper.
2 In the hot pan, fry the onion, garlic and mange-tout peas or sugar snap peas for a few minutes, until just starting to soften.

3 Add the honey, soy sauce, oyster sauce and peppercorns, and toss everything together until well mixed. Return the meat to the pan and turn the heat down. Cook for 1 minute more, and then serve.

VARIATIONS Tuna steaks could be used instead of the beef, and the vegetables can be varied for other zero-point vegetables like baby corn; strips of carrot; green beans; beansprouts or sliced peppers. Using tuna instead of beef will reduce the points to $2\frac{1}{2}$ per serving.

Honey and Black Pepper Beef: An Oriental feast for only 3½ points per serving.

Aromatic Chicken Curry: Treat yourself to a creamy curry for fewer points!

AROMATIC CHICKEN CURRY

POINTS

per recipe: 9½	per serving: 5

Serves 2
Preparation time: 15 minutes
Cooking time: 30–35 minutes
Calories per serving: 330
Freezing: recommended

Karen Shepherd is a Member from Hucknall in Nottinghamshire. She is a PhD student and also helps her husband with his business. Her favourite food is curry which is usually too high in points to fit in to her Weight Watchers Programme. Hence she has developed this recipe which has all the strong, fabulous flavours of Indian food. The secret is to use half-fat crème fraîche to keep the texture rich, but the points low.

1 tablespoon vegetable oil
1 medium onion, chopped finely
1 garlic clove, crushed
3 cm (1¼ inches) fresh ginger, grated finely
½ teaspoon turmeric
½ teaspoon ground cumin
½ teaspoon ground coriander
¼ teaspoon chilli powder
¼ teaspoon garam masala
2 ripe tomatoes, chopped
2 × 175 g (6 oz) medium boneless, skinless chicken breasts, cut into bite-sized pieces
150 ml (¼ pint) chicken stock
2 tablespoons half-fat crème fraîche
salt and freshly ground black pepper

1 Heat the oil in large saucepan, and then fry the onion and garlic for about 5 minutes until softened. Add the ginger and spices and fry for a further minute.

2 Add the tomatoes, chicken and stock. Bring to the boil, and then turn down the heat. Simmer on a medium heat for 20 minutes, until the sauce is thick and rich.

3 Turn off the heat and stir in the crème fraîche. Check the seasoning and serve.

TOP TIPS The curry tastes more fragrant if you use whole spices like coriander and cumin seeds. Grind the spices just before you use them in a pestle and mortar, or electric grinder.

You can prepare the curry in advance until step 3. Keep it in the refrigerator or freezer, and then reheat and add the crème fraîche when you want to eat it.

VARIATION Canned tomatoes or passata can be used instead of fresh tomatoes – if using passata, don't forget to add the extra points.

CHICKEN WITH ORANGE AND HONEY SAUCE

POINTS

per recipe: 9½	per serving: 5

Serves 2
Preparation time: 10 minutes + 2 hours marinating + cooling
Cooking time: 55 minutes
Calories per serving: 440
Freezing: recommended

Alison Green is a Member from Penrith in Cumbria who enjoys cooking and experimenting with recipes. She has been a Member of Weight Watchers for 19 months, and although she has spent three of those months travelling and visiting family in Australia and New Zealand she has still lost 33½ pounds. She made this recipe when she had a surplus of orange juice, and now says it's a favourite with those that come to stay in her guest house. Alison likes to serve this dish with crisp, steamed vegetables or a large green salad.

2 × 175 g (6 oz) medium skinless, boneless chicken breasts
150 ml (¼ pint) vegetable stock
300 ml (½ pint) orange juice
3 teaspoons clear honey
3 teaspoons vegetable gravy granules (optional)
salt and freshly ground black pepper

1 Preheat the oven to Gas Mark 3/ 160°C/fan oven 140°C. Make two small diagonal slits across the top of each chicken breast, and lay them in an ovenproof dish at least 5 cm (2 inches) deep.

2 Heat the stock in a small saucepan with the orange juice, honey and seasoning. Turn off the heat and leave to cool. Pour half the mixture over the chicken breasts and leave to marinate for at least 2 hours.

3 Cook the chicken in the oven for 45 minutes. Meanwhile bring the remaining mixture in the saucepan to the boil and reduce it to half the original amount.

4 Add the juices from the baked chicken to the sauce in the pan, and then add the gravy granules to thicken, if using. Pour the sauce over the cooked chicken breasts and serve.

TOP TIP This sauce is especially tasty if you use freshly squeezed orange juice.

BOBOTIE

POINTS

per recipe: 22   per serving: 5½

Serves 4
Preparation time: 15 minutes
Cooking time: 40 minutes
Calories per serving: 320
Freezing: recommended (see Top Tip)

Pam Jeffrey is a Gold Member from Stalybridge, Cheshire. She lived in Zambia in Africa for a number of years where she developed her culinary skills. This recipe is her low-fat version of the traditional South African dish. She works full-time as a civil servant and is married with two grown-up sons. She serves this dish with a mixed zero-point salad or steamed vegetables.

low-fat cooking spray
1 large onion, chopped finely
1 medium cooking apple, peeled, cored and chopped

500 g (1lb 2 oz) turkey mince
2 medium slices bread, broken into small pieces
2 tablespoons skimmed milk
1 tablespoon brown sugar
1 tablespoon wine vinegar
1 tablespoon tomato purée
1 tablespoon curry powder
50 g (1¾ oz) raisins
½ teaspoon salt
1 medium egg, beaten
juice of 1 lemon
6 bay leaves
salt and freshly ground black pepper

FOR THE TOPPING

150 ml (5 fl oz) low-fat plain yogurt
1 medium egg
1 teaspoon turmeric
salt and freshly ground black pepper

1 Preheat the oven to Gas Mark 4/180°C/fan oven 160°C. Spray a large non-stick frying pan or wok with the cooking spray, and fry the onion and apple for 5 minutes until softened – add 1 or 2 tablespoons of water if necessary to stop them sticking.

2 Add the mince to the pan, season with salt and pepper, and cook until browned. Add the bread, milk, sugar, vinegar, tomato purée, curry powder, raisins, salt, egg and lemon juice, and mix together.

3 Place the mixture in an ovenproof dish and add the bay leaves. Cover and cook in the oven for 30 minutes.

4 Meanwhile, mix the topping ingredients together in a measuring jug. Make the mixture up to 250 ml (9 fl oz) with water.

5 Remove the dish from the oven and pour over the topping. Return it, uncovered, to the oven for a further 10 minutes until the topping has set.

TOP TIP Freeze this dish without the topping. When you are ready to eat it, heat through and then add the topping as in steps 4 and 5.

VARIATION Extra-lean minced beef or lamb could be used instead of the turkey but the points per serving would increase to 7 and 8 respectively.

SHEEK KEBABS

POINTS

per recipe: 19   per serving: 5

Serves 4
Preparation and cooking time:
20 minutes
Calories per serving: 200
Freezing: recommended

Wendy Murphy is a Member from Preston in Lancashire who joined Weight Watchers with her sister and daughter because she says it works! She serves these with a salad.

400 g (14 oz) minced lamb
1 medium egg
3 garlic cloves, crushed
1 teaspoon mint sauce
2 teaspoons paprika
2 teaspoons curry powder
2 teaspoons chilli powder
1 teaspoon turmeric
1 teaspoon ground coriander
1 teaspoon ground cumin
a small bunch of fresh coriander, chopped
salt and freshly ground black pepper

1 Mix all the ingredients together in a bowl, and then divide the mixture into 12 portions. Roll each portion in your hands and then flatten slightly to make 12 kebab shapes.

2 Grill the kebabs for 5 minutes on each side, until cooked through and golden. Serve immediately, allowing three kebabs per person.

SPICY JAMBALAYA

POINTS

per recipe: 17½   per serving: 4½

Serves 4
Preparation time: 20 minutes
Cooking time: 30 minutes
Calories per serving: 365
Freezing: not recommended

Joanne Nicholls is a Member from
Great Barr in Birmingham. She
joined Weight Watchers in February
2001 to lose weight in time for her
wedding in September 2002. This
recipe is one of her mother's that she
has adapted to be spicier and low-
fat. She likes to serve it in big bowls
with a zero-point salad.

1 × 175 g (6 oz) boneless, skinless
chicken breast, chopped into bite-size
chunks
3 tablespoons Cajun spice mix
low-fat cooking spray
1 medium onion, chopped
2 garlic cloves, crushed
1 fresh red chilli, de-seeded and
chopped finely
1 yellow and 1 red pepper, de-seeded
and chopped
850 ml (1½ pints) chicken or
vegetable stock
80 g pack of sliced chorizo
400 g can of chopped tomatoes
200 g (7 oz) long-grain rice
salt and freshly ground black pepper

1 Place the chicken breast in a small
bowl and sprinkle over the Cajun spice
mix. Toss together and set aside.

2 Spray a large frying pan or wok with
the cooking spray. Add the chicken
and stir-fry for 4 minutes. Stir in the
onion, garlic, chilli and peppers, and
fry for another 4 minutes until they are
slightly browned and softened.

3 Add the stock, chorizo, tomatoes
and rice, and then bring it all to the
boil. Turn down the heat and simmer
for 20 minutes until the rice is
cooked, and has absorbed all the
liquid. Season to taste, and serve.

TOP TIP To make your own Cajun
spice mix, combine together 1
teaspoon each of paprika, ground
black pepper, ground cumin seeds,
cayenne pepper, ground mustard
seeds, dried thyme, dried oregano
and salt.

Add more chilli to the dish if you
like your food especially hot.

THAI COCONUT COD WITH FRUITED PILAU RICE

POINTS

per recipe: 11½   per serving: 6

Serves 2
Preparation time: 10 minutes
Cooking time: 20 minutes
Calories per serving: 385
Freezing: not recommended

Lisa Hall from Ealing in London has
been a Member of Weight Watchers
both here and in America for many
years now. This recipe reflects how
she likes to 'slim' her favourite flavours.
She loves the Thai coconut flavour
but could not justify the points of
creamed coconut. She developed this
dish instead using coconut essence,
available in the bakery sections of
large supermarkets.

1 tablespoon cornflour
2 tablespoons dry sherry
1 tablespoon half-fat crème fraîche
1 teaspoon green or red curry paste
1 garlic clove, crushed
¼ teaspoon coconut essence
2 × 150 g (5½ oz) cod fillets
salt and freshly ground black pepper

FOR THE RICE
50 g (1¾ oz) basmati rice
1 medium carrot, grated
2 spring onions, sliced
2 pieces of Chinese stem ginger in
syrup, chopped finely
1 tablespoon sultanas
a small bunch of fresh parsley, chopped
1 teaspoon ground coriander
1 tablespoon toasted flaked almonds

1 Preheat the oven to Gas Mark 4/
180°C/fan oven 160°C. Line a baking
sheet with a large piece of foil –
enough to make a parcel for the fish.

2 Mix the cornflour with the sherry
to make a smooth paste. Add the
crème fraîche, the curry paste, garlic
and coconut essence.

3 Season the cod with salt and
pepper, and place in the foil. Pour
over the crème fraîche mixture and
seal up the edges to make a parcel.
Bake in the oven for 20 minutes.

4 Meanwhile cook the rice as
directed on the packet, and then
drain well. Add all the remaining
ingredients to the rice, season and
toss together. Divide the rice between
two plates, and serve with the cod
and its sauce.

VARIATIONS Try this recipe with
other fish or shellfish like haddock,
salmon, tuna or prawns. Don't forget
to adjust the points accordingly.

If you are really hungry, try adding
more vegetables to the rice, such
as grated courgettes.

1 Heat the oil in a large frying pan. Add the pork steaks and season. Fry for about 5 minutes on each side until cooked through and golden brown. Remove from the pan to four serving plates and keep warm.

2 Add the onion and garlic to the pan. Cover and cook on a low heat for 5 minutes until softened. Add the mushrooms and turn the heat up. Stir-fry for 2 minutes, and then add the peppercorns, parsley, mustard and wine.

3 Allow the wine to bubble rapidly for 1 minute and then take the pan off the heat. Stir in the cream. Serve the sauce poured over the pork steaks.

TOP TIP You can buy green peppercorns either dried (in which case it is preferable to crack them before using) or bottled in brine.

VARIATION You can use whatever mushrooms are available such as button, closed cup or chestnut. Try wild mushrooms such as chanterelles for a special treat.

Pork with Creamy Mushroom and Peppercorn Sauce: A delicious sauce to complement pork.

PORK WITH CREAMY MUSHROOM AND PEPPERCORN SAUCE

POINTS	
per recipe: 15½	per serving: 4

Serves 4

Preparation and cooking time: 30 minutes

Calories per serving: 220

Freezing: not recommended

Shona MacKenzie, a Member from Inverness, rejoined Weight Watchers to lose weight for her wedding. She is very fond of cooking, and not only appreciates the motivation that she draws from her Leader, Jo, but also likes the Weight Watchers Programme as it allows her to eat and cook the food she enjoys. She finds the points system easy to use when developing her own recipes to suit her taste.

1 tablespoon vegetable oil

400 g (14 oz) thin-cut pork loin steaks (approximately 12), all fat removed

1 medium onion, chopped finely

1 garlic clove, crushed

175 g (6 oz) mushrooms, sliced

1 teaspoon green peppercorns

2 teaspoons dried or fresh parsley, chopped

1 teaspoon Dijon mustard

100 ml (3½ fl oz) dry white wine

4 tablespoons single cream

salt and freshly ground black pepper

MOROCCAN STUFFED PLAICE

POINTS

per recipe: 11	per serving: $5\frac{1}{2}$

Serves 2
Preparation time: 10 minutes
Cooking time: 30 minutes
Calories per serving: 455
Freezing: not recommended

Pat Boddy from Croft in Warrington recently joined Weight Watchers with her husband. They both enjoy cooking but have very busy lives, so this quick and tasty stuffed plaice, full of wonderful flavours of herbs and spices, is one of their favourites.

1 small onion, chopped finely

2 medium carrots, grated

a small bunch of fresh mint, chopped

1 teaspoon chilli sauce

1 garlic clove, crushed

1 teaspoon ground turmeric

$\frac{1}{2}$ teaspoon dried ginger

2 tablespoons low-fat plain yogurt

2 medium-sized plaice fillets

400 g can of chopped tomatoes

125 g ($4\frac{1}{2}$ oz) couscous

300 ml ($\frac{1}{2}$ pint) hot vegetable stock

salt and freshly ground black pepper

1 Preheat the oven to Gas Mark 4/ 180°C/fan oven 160°C. In a large bowl mix the onion, carrots, mint, chilli sauce, garlic, spices and yogurt to make the stuffing.

2 Place a large piece of kitchen foil on a baking tray – large enough to fold over the fish to make a parcel – and lay the plaice fillets in the middle. Spoon the stuffing over each fish. Carefully fold over the fillets to encase the filling.

3 Pour the tomatoes over the fish. Season and make a loose parcel with the foil, scrunching and folding the edges so that the fish is sealed in. Bake in the oven for 30 minutes.

4 About 5 minutes before the fish is ready, place the couscous in a bowl and pour over the stock – make sure it is boiling hot. Cover and leave for 5 minutes, and then fluff up with a fork. Serve the couscous with the fish and spoon over the juices from inside the foil parcel.

TOP TIP Use a teaspoon of mint sauce if there is no fresh mint available.

VARIATIONS Try using courgettes instead of carrots, and fresh coriander instead of mint. The points will remain the same.

Moroccan Stuffed Plaice: So many flavours – so few points!

FISH PIE WITH POTATO TOPPING

POINTS

per recipe: $18\frac{1}{2}$ per serving: $4\frac{1}{2}$

Serves 4
Preparation time: 30 minutes
Cooking time: 20 minutes
Calories per serving: 295
Freezing: recommended

Pippa Smith is a Member from North London. She is a full-time mum who joined Weight Watchers to get back to her pre-pregnancy weight. She finds the points system easy to follow and likes to adapt her own recipes so she can continue to eat normally. Pippa's mum made this fish pie for her when she was a child, and now Pippa adds her own Weight Watchers adaptations and a crushed potato topping for an unusual twist. She usually serves it with a salad or green vegetables.

350 g (12 oz) smoked haddock
1 teaspoon Marigold bouillon powder, or a fish or vegetable stock cube
100 g (3½ oz) fresh or frozen peas
100 g (3½ oz) carrots, diced
2 medium tomatoes, skinned, de-seeded and chopped
500 g (1lb 2 oz) new potatoes
1 teaspoon olive oil
4 tablespoons fresh white breadcrumbs
2 tablespoons grated Parmesan cheese
salt and freshly ground black pepper

FOR THE PARSLEY SAUCE

300 ml (½ pint) skimmed milk
2 tablespoons cornflour
2 tablespoons chopped fresh parsley

1 Put the haddock in a frying pan with enough water to cover it. Add the bouillon powder or stock cube, and poach the fish for 5 minutes until just cooked. Drain and leave to cool a little, and then remove the skin and flake the flesh into a large bowl.

2 Meanwhile boil the peas and carrots in lightly salted water for 3 minutes, until just tender. Drain and add to the flaked fish along with the tomatoes.

3 Cook the potatoes in plenty of lightly salted, boiling water and while they are cooking make the parsley sauce.

4 Mix 1 tablespoon of the milk with the cornflour in a small bowl to make a paste. Heat the rest of the milk in a saucepan with the parsley and some seasoning until it is just boiling. Add the cornflour paste and stir until the sauce thickens.

5 Preheat the oven to Gas Mark 5/ 190°C/fan oven 170°C. Drain and crush the cooked potatoes lightly with a fork. Stir in the olive oil, seasoning, breadcrumbs and Parmesan cheese.

6 Spoon the fish into an ovenproof dish approximately 18 cm × 25 cm (7 inches × 10 inches). Pour the parsley sauce over the fish and top with the potatoes. Bake for 20 minutes, until hot all the way through and the topping is golden and crunchy.

VARIATIONS Add a large, chopped hard-boiled egg to the fish mixture. This will add an extra ½ point per serving.

Add 40 g (1½ oz) grated half-fat Cheddar cheese to the parsley sauce, this will add an extra 1 point per serving.

Try fresh dill or fennel instead of the parsley in the sauce. The points will remain the same.

Fish Pie with
Potato Topping:
ideal for serving
to family and
friends – they'll
never know it's
so low in points!

MEDITERRANEAN CHICKEN

POINTS

per recipe: 13   per serving: 3½

Serves 4
Preparation time: 30 minutes
Cooking time: 1 hour
Calories per serving: 260
Freezing: recommended

Janet Mason is a Member from Dunstable in Bedfordshire who joined Weight Watchers in May 2001. She works at her local hospital as a PA to the Litigation Advisor and has two children aged 19 and 21. She has cooked this recipe on many occasions for friends, and has found both the weight-conscious and the not-so-conscious enjoyed it immensely.

low-fat cooking spray
4 × 175 g (6 oz) medium boneless, skinless chicken breasts
225 g (8 oz) shallots, peeled but left whole
2 garlic cloves, crushed
400 g can of chopped tomatoes
1 medium green pepper, chopped
10 black olives, chopped
a small bunch of fresh oregano, chopped, or 2 teaspoons dried oregano
1 tablespoon red wine vinegar
1 tablespoon tomato purée
1 teaspoon artificial sweetener
150 ml (¼ pint) dry white wine
zest of 1 lemon
1 tablespoon capers
a small bunch of fresh basil, chopped
salt and freshly ground black pepper

1 Preheat the oven to Gas Mark 2/ 150°C/fan oven 130°C. Heat a large frying pan and spray with the cooking spray. Season and fry the chicken breasts until golden. Transfer the chicken to a casserole dish.

2 In the same frying pan, fry the shallots and garlic for 2 minutes, until they start to brown. Add the tomatoes, pepper, olives, oregano, vinegar, tomato purée, sweetener, white wine and seasoning.

3 Bring to the boil and stir together well, scraping up any stuck-on juices with a wooden spoon. Pour the sauce over the chicken in the casserole dish. Cover and cook in the oven for 1 hour.

4 Remove the dish from the oven and check the seasoning. Sprinkle with the lemon zest, capers and chopped basil, and serve.

VARIATION Chicken thighs or legs could be used instead of the chicken breasts, but remember to alter the points accordingly.

BEEF AND APRICOT STEW

POINTS

per recipe: 14   per serving: 3½

Serves 4
Preparation time: 30 minutes
Cooking time: 1 hour
Calories per serving: 225
Freezing: recommended

Sarah Dolby, a Member from Melton Mowbray in Leicestershire, is a full-time mum with two young children. She has carefully adapted this recipe from the full-fat version using low-fat cooking spray and very lean meat. She often serves it as a Sunday meal with dry-roast potatoes and green beans.

low-fat cooking spray
1 large onion, chopped finely
450 g (1 lb) lean stewing beef, diced
2 medium carrots, chopped
200 g (7 oz) button mushrooms, cleaned
125 ml (4 fl oz) vegetable stock
2 teaspoons ground cinnamon or 1 cinnamon stick
50 g (1¾ oz) dried apricots, halved
2 teaspoons dried rosemary or 1 sprig of fresh rosemary
1 tablespoon cornflour, mixed to a thin paste with 3 tablespoons water
salt and freshly ground black pepper

1 Preheat the oven to Gas Mark 4/ 180°C/fan oven 160°C. Spray a large frying pan or wok with the low-fat cooking spray. Fry the onion for 5 minutes until softened, adding a little water if necessary to prevent it sticking.

2 Add the beef, season with salt and pepper, and stir-fry until browned all over. Add the carrots, mushrooms, stock, ground cinnamon or cinnamon stick, apricots and rosemary. Bring to the boil, and then stir in the cornflour to thicken the sauce.

3 Pour into an ovenproof dish, cover with a lid and cook in the oven, for 1 hour. Season to taste, and then serve.

VARIATION You could also try using four shallots instead of the onion. Leave out the apricots and cinnamon and then substitute 125 ml (4 fl oz) red wine for the same quantity of stock. The points per serving will remain the same.

MEXICAN SWORDFISH WITH SPICY SALSA

Serves 2
Preparation and cooking time:
25 minutes + 1 hour marinating
Calories per serving: 255
Freezing: not recommended

Sarah Nicholls is a Member from
Eastwood in Nottingham. She is
married, works as a personnel
administrator and enjoys swimming
and golf. Although Sarah is not
usually a big fish eater, this recipe
appealed to her and she thought
she'd try it out. She has since
adapted it to her own taste.
Sarah says this dish is delicious
accompanied by a jacket potato or
dry-roasted potato wedges, adding
on the extra points.

2 × 150 g (5¹/₂ oz) swordfish steaks
(see Variations for alternatives)

zest and juice of 2 limes

a small bunch of fresh coriander,
chopped

salt and freshly ground black pepper

FOR THE SALSA

1 medium mango, skinned and diced

1 teaspoon chilli paste

1 small red onion, chopped finely

3 medium tomatoes, quartered,
de-seeded and chopped

1 Marinate the swordfish steaks in
the lime zest and juice, and half the
coriander for 1 hour.

2 Meanwhile mix together all the
salsa ingredients with the remaining
coriander in a serving bowl.

3 Season the swordfish steaks. Cook
them under a hot grill or on a hot
griddle for 4–5 minutes on each side,
until just cooked through and golden
on the outside. Serve the fish with
the salsa.

TOP TIP This dish is great cooked
on the barbecue.

VARIATIONS For a change, try
marlin, shark or tuna steaks –
varying the points accordingly.

**Mexican Swordfish
with Spicy Salsa:
Treat yourself to
some exotic
flavours.**

It appears that many of you are turning your hand to vegetarian cooking, whether for yourselves or for a family member. Vegetarian meals are now becoming part of the weekly menu and these recipes illustrate how innovative and imaginative Weight Watchers Members are with veggie cooking. Ideal for families, these recipes will fill hungry tummies without anyone even noticing that meat is missing. Not only will they fill you up and keep off the pounds, but they are super-healthy too.

BUTTERNUT SQUASH & BEAN CHILLI

POINTS

per recipe: $17\frac{1}{2}$ per serving: $4\frac{1}{2}$

V *if using vegetarian cheese*
Serves 4
Preparation time: 30 minutes
Cooking time: 30 minutes
Calories per serving: 240
Freezing: recommended

Linda Ratcliffe is a Leader from Borough Green in Kent. She first joined Weight Watchers back in 1992 since she'd put on 4 stone during pregnancy. After having a glamorous PR career in the film industry, she lost all her self-esteem. She reached her Goal in 1994, but after a couple of years the weight crept back on again. Determined to be slim for her 50th birthday, she rejoined Weight Watchers. She lost three stone and went on to become a Leader. She loves this recipe as it is so filling, healthy and, above all, low in points. Linda serves this dish with crusty bread, adding the extra points.

1 medium butternut squash, peeled and cut into large chunks
low-fat cooking spray
2 garlic cloves, chopped
2 fresh red chillies, de-seeded and chopped
1 × 420 g can of red kidney beans
1 × 300 g can of cannellini beans
1 × 300 g can of flageolet beans
425 ml (3/4 pint) vegetable stock
a small bunch of fresh coriander, chopped
1 teaspoon cornflour
40 g (1 1/2 oz) half-fat mature Cheddar cheese, grated
salt and freshly ground black pepper

1 Preheat the oven to Gas Mark 6/ 200°C/fan oven 180°C. Bake the chunks of butternut squash for 20 minutes.

2 Meanwhile place a 2 litre (3½-pint) flameproof casserole dish on the hob. Spray with the cooking spray, and then fry the garlic and chillies for half a minute. Add the beans, stock, coriander and seasoning, and stir together.

3 Mix the cornflour with a little water to make a paste, and then stir it into the bean mixture. Finally add the half-baked squash to the casserole dish. Cover and cook in the oven for 20 minutes.

4 Remove the dish from the oven and sprinkle over the cheese. Return to the oven, leaving the lid off, for a further 10 minutes.

VARIATIONS This dish is good served with couscous, rice or boiled potatoes. Remember to add the extra points.

Butternut
Squash and
Bean Chilli:
So tasty and
satisfying for
only 4½ points
per serving.

ROAST VEGETABLE LASAGNE

POINTS

per recipe: 30   per serving: 5

(v) if using vegetarian cheese
Serves 6
Preparation time: 30 minutes
Cooking time: 1 hour
Calories per serving: 300
Freezing: recommended

Mrs Diane Mobbs is a Gold Member from Handforth in Cheshire. She has created a fantastic low-point version of lasagne.

1 medium courgette, cut into chunks
1 medium red and 1 medium yellow pepper, de-seeded and sliced
1 large carrot, cut into chunks
1 medium leek, sliced
6 medium tomatoes, quartered
1 garlic clove, chopped
2 teaspoons sesame oil

1 × 455 g jar of reduced-fat tomato pasta sauce
9 sheets no need to pre-cook lasagne verdi
150 g (5½ oz) half-fat Cheddar cheese, grated
salt and freshly ground black pepper

FOR THE BÉCHAMEL SAUCE

600 ml (1 pint) skimmed milk
½ medium carrot, unpeeled
½ medium onion
8 peppercorns
4 cloves
1 teaspoon ground mace
1 bay leaf
30 g (1¼ oz) plain white flour
2 teaspoons polyunsaturated margarine

1 Preheat the oven to Gas Mark 6/ 200°C/fan oven 180°C. Place all the vegetables and garlic in a roasting dish. Season, sprinkle with sesame oil. Toss them together. Roast for 30 minutes until the vegetables are tender and crispy around the edges.

2 Meanwhile make the béchamel sauce. Heat the milk in a saucepan with the carrot, onion, peppercorns, cloves, mace and bay leaf. Bring to the boil, then turn off the heat. Leave for 15 minutes before straining.

3 In a medium saucepan whisk together the flour, margarine and a few tablespoons of the infused milk to make a paste. Add the rest of the milk and turn on the heat. Bring to the boil whisking continuously. Turn down the heat. Simmer for 5 minutes until smooth and thick. Season.

4 Combine the roasted vegetables with the tomato pasta sauce. Use a third of the vegetable mixture to cover the bottom of a 30 cm × 23 cm (12-inch × 9-inch) ovenproof dish.

5 Top the mixture with three sheets of lasagne, just under a third of the sauce and a handful of grated cheese. Repeat the layers twice, ending with a large third of sauce, and the remaining cheese.

6 Bake in the oven for 25–30 minutes, until cooked through and golden.

FRUITY VEG STIR-FRY

POINTS

per recipe: 4½   per serving: 2½

(v) Serves 2
Preparation and cooking time: 20 minutes
Calories per serving: 195
Freezing: recommended

Mrs Angela Franklin is a Member from Far Cotton in Northamptonshire. She is a working mother of three who joined Weight Watchers 11 weeks ago through fear of reaching 40, and being too old and overweight to enjoy life to the full. She has already lost 19½ pounds. This recipe was created by thinking of all her favourite zero-point foods and finding complementary ones. Serve with half a warm pitta bread.

1 teaspoon vegetable oil
1 garlic clove, crushed
12 button mushrooms, halved
6 cherry tomatoes, halved
6 spring onions, chopped into 2.5 cm (1-inch) lengths
1 medium red, 1 medium green and 1 medium yellow pepper, sliced
100 g (3½ oz) pineapple (about 3 rings from the can), chopped
juice from 432 g can of pineapple
1 cm (½-inch) piece of fresh ginger, grated
2 tablespoons soy sauce
2 teaspoons cornflour

1 Heat the oil in a large frying pan or wok until very hot, and then stir-fry the garlic, mushrooms, tomatoes, spring onions, peppers and pineapple pieces for 4 minutes.

2 Add the pineapple juice, ginger and soy sauce, and bring to the boil. Meanwhile mix the cornflour with 1 tablespoon of water to make a paste. Mix it in to the stir-fry.

3 Cook for a few more minutes until the sauce thickens, and then serve.

VARIATIONS If you want a meaty version try adding 1 × 150 g (5½ oz) shredded, skinless, cooked chicken breast to the stir-fry. Add 1½ points per serving.

Baby corn could be substituted for any of the vegetables.

 **VEGGIE COBBLER**

POINTS

per recipe: 15½   per serving: 4

Ⓥ *without the Worcestershire sauce*
Serves 4
Preparation time: 25 minutes
Cooking time: 1¼ hours
Calories per serving: 340
Freezing: recommended

Annette Beavan from Northfield in Birmingham has been a Member for five years. She originally lost 2½ stone but lapsed back when family problems arose. Now she's back attending Meetings regularly and has lost 1½ stone so far. She loves cooking including baking and cake-decorating. This recipe was given to her years ago, but she's adapted it to suit the Weight Watchers Programme. She often serves it to family and friends without anyone ever noticing that it's low-fat and low-calorie!

300 g (10½ oz) leeks, chopped

225 g (8 oz) carrots, chopped

225 g (8 oz) mushrooms, sliced

1 medium red pepper, de-seeded and chopped

1 × 400 g can of red kidney beans

1 × 400 g can of chopped tomatoes

2 tablespoons tomato purée

1 tablespoon garlic purée

100 ml (3½ fl oz) vegetable stock

2 tablespoons Worcestershire sauce

1 teaspoon mixed dried herbs

salt and freshly ground black pepper

FOR THE COBBLER TOPPING

40 g (1½ oz) polyunsaturated margarine

125 g (4½ oz) self-raising white flour

1 tablespoon mixed dried herbs

2 tablespoons skimmed milk

salt and freshly ground black pepper

1 Preheat the oven to Gas Mark 4/ 180°C/fan oven 160°C. Place all the ingredients except those for the topping in a large casserole dish. Stir to mix.

2 To make the topping, rub the margarine into the flour with your fingertips until the mixture resembles coarse breadcrumbs.

3 Add the herbs, milk and seasoning to the mixture and stir with a palette knife. Bring the mixture together with your fingertips to make a soft dough.

4 Divide the dough into eight pieces and gently roll each piece into a ball, and then flatten slightly. Arrange the dough balls around the edge of the vegetables in the casserole dish.

5 Cover, bake for 1–1¼ hours, removing the lid for the final 15 minutes and stirring the vegetables occasionally to prevent them from drying out. When ready, the stew will be reduced and thick and the cobbler will be risen and golden on top.

TOP TIP Handle the dough as little as possible or it will become tough.

VARIATION Use any zero-point vegetables.

Veggie Cobbler: Delicious dough balls!

**Sausage Casserole
with Leek and
Onion Mash:
An amazing 5 points
per serving.**

SAUSAGE CASSEROLE WITH LEEK AND ONION MASH

POINTS

per recipe: 19   per serving: 5

Ⓥ Ⓥᵉ *Serves 4*
Preparation time: 20 minutes
Cooking time: 1¼ hours
Calories per serving: 365
Freezing: recommended (without the mash)

Denise Gibb is a Gold Member from Huddersfield in West Yorkshire. This recipe is one of her favourites not only because she loves Quorn sausages, but also because she can prepare it quickly in the morning and then leave it in the slow cooker.

2–3 medium carrots, chopped
1 large onion, chopped
1 garlic clove, crushed
250 g packet of Quorn sausages, halved (6 in a packet)
415 g can of baked beans
400 g can of chopped tomatoes
1 teaspoon dried mixed herbs
salt and freshly ground black pepper

FOR THE MASH

1 large leek, chopped and washed
a bunch of spring onions, chopped
4 × 200 g (7 oz) medium potatoes, cut into chunks

1 Preheat the oven (if using) to Gas Mark 2/150°C/fan oven 130°C. Place all the casserole ingredients in a flameproof casserole dish with 200 ml (7 fl oz) of water. Place the dish on the hob and bring the mixture to the boil. Then either transfer to the oven for an hour, or turn the heat down low and leave it on the hob for an hour.

2 Half an hour before you are ready to eat, place the leek, spring onions and potatoes in a large pan with enough lightly salted boiling water just to cover them. Cook them for 20 minutes or until tender. Drain and mash together with some seasoning. Serve the casserole with the leek and onion mash.

TOP TIP To reduce the points replace the baked beans with zero-point vegetables such as celery, celeriac, cabbage, Brussels sprouts, swede or turnips. This will reduce the points by 1½ per serving.

LENTIL PATTIES

POINTS

per recipe: 8   per serving: 2

Ⓥ *Serves 4*
Preparation time: 10 minutes
Cooking time: 25 minutes
Calories per serving: 150
Freezing: recommended

Lyle Brookes is a Gold Member from Tenbury Wells in Worcestershire. She is a widow aged 73 with three daughters, two of whom are vegetarians. She has been making this recipe for about 15 years now and finds it is especially popular with her 17 year-old grandson. It is easy to make, economical, nutritious and delicious.

400 g can of chopped tomatoes
1 medium onion, chopped finely
100 g (3½ oz) split red lentils, rinsed
50 g (1¾ oz) raisins
1 teaspoon curry powder
a small bunch of fresh parsley, chopped
juice of 1 lemon
1 tablespoon plain white flour
low-fat cooking spray
salt and freshly ground black pepper

1 Put the tomatoes in a medium-sized saucepan, and add the onion and lentils. Cover and cook for 15 minutes, stirring to avoid the mixture sticking – adding a small quantity of water if the mixture is dry but the lentils are not yet soft.
2 Stir in the raisins, curry powder, parsley, lemon juice and seasoning, and cook for a further 5 minutes. Leave to cool.
3 When cool, shape the mixture into four flat patties and coat them lightly in flour.

4 Heat a large frying pan and spray with the cooking spray. Fry each patty over a low heat for 5 minutes on each side. Serve the lentil patties hot or cold.

Lentil Patties: Delicious with 1 tablespoon of chutney for 1 point.

WHAT-YOU-WILL RISOTTO

POINTS

per recipe: 14   **per serving:** 7

Ⓥ *if using vegetarian cheese*
Serves 2
Preparation time: 10 minutes
Cooking time: 25 minutes
Calories per serving: 500
Freezing: not recommended

Pat Holbrook is a Member from Stretton in Warrington. She has only just joined Weight Watchers, but has already lost a satisfying amount and feels confident that she'll reach her Goal. Pat especially likes this recipe because it is so flexible. Her husband gets the lion's share and she supplements her portion with a large fresh, zero-point salad.

1 tablespoon olive oil
3 spring onions, sliced
1 garlic clove, crushed
200 g (7 oz) risotto rice
850 ml (1½ pints) hot vegetable stock
15 g (½ oz) porcini mushrooms, soaked in 150 ml (¼ pint) hot water
250 g (9 oz) mushrooms, sliced
2 sprigs fresh thyme or a pinch of dried thyme
1 tablespoon Parmesan cheese, grated finely
a small bunch of fresh parsley, chopped
salt and freshly ground black pepper

1 Heat the oil in a large frying pan and fry the spring onions and garlic for 1 minute. Add the rice and stir to coat it in the oil.

2 Add a quarter of the stock to the pan, and bring to a simmer stirring frequently. Meanwhile drain the porcini mushrooms, but reserve the soaking liquid. Chop the porcini, and add them to the risotto with the fresh mushrooms, the soaking liquid and the thyme.

3 Continue to simmer, stirring almost continuously. When the rice has absorbed the liquid add another quarter of the stock. Continue to add stock in this way until it is all used up, and the rice is just cooked.

4 Season the risotto and stir in the Parmesan cheese and parsley before serving.

VARIATION You could try adding prawns and asparagus: add chopped asparagus spears half way through cooking and prawns just before the end. Don't forget to add the points.

QUORN AND CHICK-PEA TIKKA

POINTS

per recipe: 9   **per serving:** 2½

Ⓥ Ⓥⓖ *Serves 4*
Preparation time: 15 minutes
Cooking time: 45 minutes
Calories per serving: 245
Freezing: recommended

Mrs Dannie Wognum is a Gold Member from Chelmsford in Essex. She joined Weight Watchers in May 2000 and within a year she had lost 3 stone and reached Gold. She is a nurse who works night shifts, so she likes filling and flavoursome recipes that she can prepare quickly before work. She's also a vegetarian so this recipe meets all the criteria and is one of her favourites.

2 medium carrots, chopped
¼ Savoy cabbage, shredded
100 g (3½ oz) green beans, topped and each cut into 3 pieces
low-fat cooking spray
1 large onion, chopped
200 g (7 oz) mushrooms, sliced
150 g (5½ oz) Quorn pieces
200 g (7 oz) sweetcorn
400 g can of chick-peas, rinsed and drained
400 g can of chopped tomatoes
150 ml (¼ pint) vegetable stock
2 large tablespoons Tikka curry powder
salt and freshly ground black pepper

1 Place the carrots, cabbage and beans in a large saucepan of lightly salted boiling water and simmer for 10–15 minutes, until just soft.

2 Meanwhile spray a large frying pan or wok with the cooking spray. Fry the onion for a few minutes, until soft – adding a tablespoon or more of water to the pan if they begin to stick.

3 Add the mushrooms and Quorn pieces and stir-fry for 4–5 minutes. Add all the other ingredients to the pan including the cooked carrots, cabbage and beans.

4 Stir together, and then cover and cook on a low heat for 25 minutes, stirring from time to time. Remove the lid for the last 10 minutes turning up the heat to reduce the liquid a little and to make a rich curry.

VARIATIONS Any zero-point vegetables can be used in this dish.

Beans like haricot, kidney, butter, or lentils can be substituted for the chick-peas. Remember to adjust the points accordingly.

BAKED NUTTY STUFFED AUBERGINES

POINTS

per recipe: 7½   per serving: 4

V *if using vegetarian cheese*

Serves 2

Preparation time: 30 minutes

Cooking time: 30 minutes

Calories per serving: 295

Freezing: not recommended

Gillian Glennie is now a Gold Member having attended Weight Watchers four times since she first joined in 1975. She works as a warden to ten sheltered homes and also runs a bed and breakfast. She has nine grandchildren and in her spare time, she loves to garden and do dress-making. So far, she has lost a stone at Weight Watchers and says, this time, she has a strong resolve to stay slim. She is a vegetarian although she occasionally eats fish, and loves this recipe as it is filling and oh-so-tasty. Gillian serves this dish with brown rice or boiled potatoes remembering to add on the extra points.

1 large aubergine

2 teaspoons extra-virgin olive oil

1 medium onion, chopped finely

2 or 3 mushrooms, sliced

100 g (3½ oz) Quorn mince

2 tablespoons chopped nuts

1 garlic clove, crushed

1 teaspoon mixed dried herbs

1 teaspoon marmite

227 g can of chopped tomatoes

40 g (1½ oz) half-fat Cheddar cheese, grated

salt and freshly ground black pepper

a handful of chopped parsley, to garnish

1 Preheat the oven to Gas Mark 6/ 200°C/fan oven 180°C. Slice the aubergine in half lengthways, and then scoop out the flesh leaving 5 mm (¼ inch) inside the skin to make a firm shell. Chop the flesh finely.

2 Heat the oil in a frying pan and gently fry the aubergine flesh, onion, mushrooms and Quorn mince together for 5 minutes, until soft. Add all the other ingredients apart from the cheese and parsley garnish, and mix together.

3 Place the aubergine shells side by side in an ovenproof dish or baking tray, and then spoon the mixture equally into each one.

4 Cover the stuffed aubergines with foil and bake in the oven for 20 minutes. Remove the foil, scatter over the cheese and bake for a further 10 minutes, until the cheese is melted and golden. Sprinkle the aubergines with chopped parsley and serve.

Baked Nutty Stuffed Aubergines: An exciting way to cook aubergines.

VEGETABLE AND LENTIL MOUSSAKA

POINTS

per recipe: 8½   per serving: 2

Ⓥ *if using vegetarian cheese*
Serves 4
Preparation time: 45 minutes
Cooking time: 30 minutes
Calories per serving: 205
Freezing: recommended

Jean Parkhouse from South Wales has been a Member since June 2000. She had tried and failed to lose weight on her own but the Weight Watchers programme suited her perfectly, as her 28½-pound weight loss will testify. She loves this recipe as it is so low in points, but still very filling.

2 tablespoons large green lentils, rinsed
1 large aubergine, sliced into 5 mm (¼-inch) slices
2 teaspoons olive oil
1 large onion, chopped
1 garlic clove, crushed
3 medium carrots, sliced thinly
2 celery sticks, sliced thinly
100 g (3½ oz) mushrooms, sliced
3 medium tomatoes, skinned and chopped
1 medium courgette, sliced
300 ml (½ pint) vegetable stock
1 tablespoon tomato purée
a small bunch of fresh thyme
a small bunch of fresh basil, chopped
salt and freshly ground black pepper

FOR THE ONION AND CHIVE SAUCE

425 ml (¾ pint) skimmed milk
1 small onion, chopped finely
a small bunch of chives, chopped finely
2 tablespoons plain white flour
a grating or a pinch of nutmeg
25 g (1 oz) half-fat Cheddar cheese, grated

1 Put the lentils in a medium saucepan with plenty of lightly salted water. Bring to the boil, turn down the heat, and then simmer for 15 minutes, until the lentils are tender. Skim off any scum that comes to the surface. Drain and set aside.

2 Meanwhile, preheat the grill. Lay the slices of the aubergine on the grill pan. Season them and grill for about 10 minutes on each side, until dried out and golden.

3 Heat the oil in a large frying pan and fry the onion and garlic for 5 minutes, until softened. Add the carrots, celery, mushrooms, tomatoes and courgette, and stir-fry on a high heat for 2 minutes.

4 Add the cooked lentils, stock, tomato purée, thyme, basil and seasoning. Bring to the boil. Turn down the heat and simmer for 10 minutes until the mixture is slightly reduced and thickened.

5 Meanwhile preheat the oven to Gas Mark 5/190°C/fan oven 170°C and make the onion and chive sauce. Place all but 4 tablespoons of the milk, the onion and chives in a small saucepan and bring to the boil.

6 In a small bowl mix the remaining cold milk with the flour to make a smooth paste. Add the paste to the hot milk whisking continuously over a low heat until the sauce thickens. Season and add the nutmeg.

7 Pour the vegetable sauce into a 1.2 litre (2-pint) ovenproof dish and lay the aubergines on top. Pour over the onion and chive sauce, and sprinkle the top with the grated cheese. Bake in the oven for 30 minutes until bubbling and golden. Spoon on to four plates and serve.

TOP TIP Freeze what you don't need in small quantities ready for future use.

MUSHROOM STROGANOFF

POINTS

per recipe: 2½   per serving: ½

Ⓥ *if using vegetarian fromage frais*
Serves 4
Preparation time: 15 minutes
Cooking time: 15 minutes
Calories per serving: 45
Freezing: not recommended

Penny Tottle is a Member from Weston-Super-Mare in Somerset. Having lost 16 pounds in her first 6 weeks at Weight Watchers, she wishes she had joined years ago. She is an NVQ teacher which means she cannot always stop for lunch, so the Weight Watchers All Day Snack Bars come in very handy. With two vegetarians in the family, this recipe is a popular one.

1 large onion, chopped
2 garlic cloves, crushed
100 ml (3½ fl oz) vegetable stock
8 tablespoons very low-fat plain fromage frais
1 tablespoon tomato purée
500 g (1lb 2 oz) closed-cup mushrooms, sliced or quartered
salt and freshly ground black pepper

1 Heat a heavy-based frying pan and add the onion, garlic and stock. Cook for 10 minutes until softened.

2 Add all the other ingredients to the pan. Stir together and cook for a further 5 minutes on a low heat until warmed through, but do not boil.

VARIATION The amounts of onion, garlic and tomato can all be varied to suit your taste.

Vegetable and Lentil Moussaka: Mouth-watering moussaka for only 2 points per serving.

Boozy Berry Sundaes: Superb sundaes for only 3½ points per serving.

desserts

Here's where we cut to the chase ... the puddings. It's obvious from the wealth of delicious entries in this category that you, the Members, are not going to let your Weight Loss Programmes get in the way of your enjoyment of food and, in particular, your enjoyment of sweet desserts. All the recipes in this chapter have been developed with the sole aim of satisfying those with a sweet tooth with the minimum of points – and they work!

BOOZY BERRY SUNDAES

POINTS	
per recipe: 13	per serving: 3½

Serves 4
Preparation and cooking time:
15 minutes + 2 hours cooling
Calories per serving: 170
Freezing: not recommended

Mrs Phyllis Dawson is a Member from Penistone in South Yorkshire. She is a 67 year-old mother of three and grandmother of four. Her hobbies include painting, cross-stitch and baking. She used to make this trifle before becoming a Member – but then she adapted it into a Weight Watcher-friendly version.

2½ tablespoons blancmange powder (strawberry or raspberry flavour)

1 tablespoon artificial sweetener

425 ml (³/₄ pint) semi-skimmed milk

2 meringue nests

225 g (8 oz) summer berries, such as strawberries or raspberries

1 tablespoon brandy (optional)

4 tablespoons half-fat crème fraîche

½ Cadbury's chocolate flake (about 5 cm/2 inches)

1 In a medium-sized saucepan mix the blancmange powder with the sweetener and a little milk to make a paste. Add the rest of the milk and bring to the boil. Turn down the heat and stir for about 5 minutes until the blancmange is thickened. Leave to cool for 2 hours.

2 Take four serving glasses and crumble half a meringue into each one. Divide the fruit between each glass. Sprinkle over the brandy, if using, and spoon on the cool blancmange mixture.

3 Finish each sundae with a tablespoon of crème fraîche and a crumbling of chocolate flake.

VARIATION To make Black Forest Sundaes, substitute the cherries for the summer berries and chocolate blancmange for the strawberry flavour. The points will remain the same.

MELBA SURPRISE

POINTS

per recipe: 6	per serving: 1½

Ⓥ *if using free-range eggs*

Serves 4

Preparation time: 10 minutes

Cooking time: 25–30 minutes

Calories per serving: 120

Freezing: not recommended

Carol Allen is a Gold Member from Alwoodley in Leeds. She is a mother of two teenage children and became a Gold Member when her second child was a baby. She has struggled over the years to maintain her weight, but finds the Weight Watchers points programme invaluable as it allows for such a flexible diet. This recipe was developed one wet afternoon when she and her daughter were at a loose end, and decided to make a dessert using her daughter's favourite – meringue. The surprise was that the whole family enjoyed it including her fussy son!

Melba Surprise: Marvellous meringue.

4 medium peaches
100 g (3½ oz) raspberries, fresh or frozen
50 ml (2 fl oz) apple or orange juice
2 medium egg whites
50 g (1¾ oz) caster sugar

1 Preheat the oven to Gas Mark 4/ 180°C/fan oven 160°C. Cut the peaches in half and remove the stones. Lay them in the bottom of a 20 cm (8-inch) ovenproof flan dish.
2 Sprinkle over the raspberries and fruit juice. Bake in the oven for 15 minutes, until the peaches begin to soften.
3 Meanwhile whisk the egg whites until very firm, stiff and dry. Whisk in the sugar in two lots to make a thick, glossy meringue mixture.
4 Spoon the meringue mixture over the fruit. Return to the oven for a further 10–15 minutes, until the meringue is a light golden colour. Serve the dish hot, straight from the oven.

TOP TIP To make a successful meringue use egg whites at room temperature rather than straight from the fridge. Always make sure that the bowl and whisk are scrupulously clean and dry before use.

VARIATIONS Other good fruit combinations are: mango and raspberries; passion fruit and peaches or strawberries and blackberries.

FRUIT BRÛLÉE

POINTS

per recipe: 6	per serving: 1½

Ⓥ *Serves 4*

Preparation and cooking time: 10 minutes + 30 minutes chilling

Calories per serving: 110

Freezing not recommended:

Maureen Molloy is a Member from Palmers Green in London. She joined Weight Watchers in January 2001 and, so far, she has lost 2 stone. Her husband and three grown-up children are very supportive and enjoy all the different recipes she makes from the Weight Watchers cookbooks. Maureen created this simple dessert because she is allergic to cream and wanted a quick, but good-looking sweet to serve.

125 g (4½ oz) blueberries
125 g (4½ oz) redcurrants
artificial sweetener (optional)
15 ml (½ fl oz) Drambuie or other liqueur
300 ml (10 fl oz) low-fat set plain Bio yogurt
4 heaped teaspoons demerara sugar

1 Divide the fruit between four ramekin dishes and sprinkle with artificial sweetener, if using. Pour over the liqueur and then spoon on the yogurt. Refrigerate for 30 minutes.
2 Preheat the grill to the highest setting. Top each ramekin with a heaped teaspoon of demerara sugar and grill for 1–2 minutes, until the sugar is bubbling and golden. Chill until ready to serve.

Fruit Brûlée:
This is also
delicious served
hot, straight
from the grill.

**Fresh Strawberry
Ice Cream:
A miraculous 1½
points per serving.**

FRESH STRAWBERRY ICE CREAM

POINTS

per recipe: 10   per serving: 1½

Ⓥ Serves 8

Preparation time: 10 minutes + 20 minutes in an ice cream maker

Calories per serving: 85

Freezing: recommended

Amanda Macrae is a Leader from Southend Common near Henley-on-Thames. She joined Weight Watchers and lost 53 pounds to reach her Goal, and then went on to become a Leader. She has always been very interested in food and inventing new recipes. Ice cream is one of her favourites, and so she set about creating an acceptably low-point version that both Weight Watchers and her other friends would enjoy.

| 600 ml (1 pint) low-fat custard |
| 150 ml (5 fl oz) 0% fat Greek yogurt |
| 200 g (7 oz) strawberries |
| 1 teaspoon caster sugar |

---

1 Mix the custard and yogurt together in a large mixing bowl. Purée the strawberries in a blender or push them through a sieve.
2 Mix the strawberries and sugar with the custard and yogurt mixture, and then pour into the ice cream maker. Churn for 20 minutes until frozen.

3 Store in the freezer in a suitable airtight container. Remove the ice cream from the freezer 10 minutes before you want to serve it.

TOP TIP If you do not have an ice cream maker pour the mixture straight into a freezer container and freeze for an hour, and then remove it and beat with a fork to break up the forming ice crystals. Freeze for another half an hour, and then beat again. Continue to do this at half-hour intervals until frozen.

VARIATIONS Substitute any summer soft fruit or a mixture of fruits.

FIRED STRAWBERRIES

POINTS

per recipe: 2   per serving: ½

Ⓥ Ⓥ₉ Serves 4

Preparation and cooking time: 15 minutes

Calories per serving: 40

Freezing: not recommended

Siobhan McCrory is a Gold Member from Bishopthorpe in York. She finds it enormously important to maintain her weight as she eats for a living! She works in product development, and is responsible for developing the recipes for ready meals for all the major retailers. As a result she is constantly travelling, staying in hotels and trying out new foods. Despite all this eating, she still wants to stay slim which is where Weight Watchers comes in – and succeeds. These strawberries are great served with Weight Watchers ice cream, but remember to add the extra points.

| 400 g (14 oz) strawberries, hulled |
| juice and zest of 1 large orange |
| 2 teaspoons cinnamon |

---

1 Place the strawberries in the centre of a large foil square approximately 30 cm × 30 cm (12 inches × 12 inches) and sprinkle over the orange juice, zest and cinnamon.

2 Fold up the foil to make a parcel which seals in the juice and the fruit. Place under a preheated grill, or on a hot barbecue or griddle pan for 10 minutes, until the strawberries are soft and the juice turned to syrup.
3 Unfold the parcel and spoon on to serving plates immediately.

VARIATIONS Try other soft fruit such as raspberries or blackberries, or try tropical or stone fruits like mangoes, papaya, pineapple, plums or peaches.

RASPBERRY FLUFF

POINTS

per recipe: 8	per serving: 2

V *if using vegetarian fromage frais*
Serves 4
Preparation time and cooking time:
20 minutes
Calories per serving: 140
Freezing: not recommended

Christine Hird is a Member from Sidcup in Kent. She has a busy household with her husband, two sons, both in their twenties, and her pets – 2 dogs, 2 parrots, 4 lovebirds, 12 tortoises, 1 snake and countless Koi in her pond! This recipe originally made with double cream and honey, had long been a family favourite. After joining Weight Watchers and successfully losing 34 pounds, Christine adapted it to fit in to her Programme – and still thinks it's great.

100 g (3½ oz) oatmeal

175 g (6 oz) fresh raspberries

2–3 teaspoons artificial sweetener

175 g (6 oz) very low-fat plain fromage frais

1 tablespoon whisky

mint sprigs, to decorate

1 Toast the oatmeal under the grill for 2–3 minutes until golden, but do not let it burn or it will taste bitter. Leave to cool.

2 In a large bowl mix the raspberries with a teaspoon of sweetener, but reserve a few for decoration. Add the fromage frais, whisky and the rest of the sweetener to taste.

3 Layer the raspberry mixture with the oatmeal in four serving glasses. Decorate with the reserved raspberries and mint sprigs, and serve at once.

STRAWBERRY CHEESECAKE

POINTS

per recipe: 20½	per serving: 2

Serves 10
Preparation time: 30 minutes
+ 1½ hours chilling time
Calories per serving: 100
Freezing: not recommended

Anita Pitman from Chichester in West Sussex has been a Member since May 1997. Although she reached her Goal weight by December of the same year, a three-week holiday in Canada where sugar and fat-laden food was everywhere, put a stone back on. Thanks to Weight Watchers she's now back at her Goal and loves to experiment with cooking Weight Watchers style at home. She works as a cost controller for a large hotel in Goodwood Park.

100 g (3½ oz) low-fat digestive biscuits, crushed

1 medium egg white, whisked lightly

2 × sachets no-sugar strawberry jelly

2 × 200 g tub of low-fat soft cheese

1 × 200 g pot of Mullerlite strawberry yogurt

100 g (3½ oz) fresh strawberries, hulled and halved

1 In a bowl mix the crushed biscuits with the whisked egg white. Tip the mixture into a high-sided 20 cm (8-inch) loose-bottomed round cake tin and press it down with your fingers, or the back of a metal spoon, to make a base. Place in the refrigerator for 30 minutes to harden.

2 Make up one of the jellies using just 150 ml (¼ pint) of boiling water, and then leave to cool slightly.

3 Meanwhile, beat together the soft cheese and yogurt in a bowl, and add the prepared jelly. Beat together until well mixed. Alternatively you can blend the cheese, yogurt and jelly in a blender or food processor.

4 Pour the cheese mixture on to the biscuit base. Place the cheesecake in the refrigerator for about 30 minutes, until set.

5 Meanwhile, make up the other jelly as instructed on the packet and leave it to cool – do not put it in the refrigerator as you do not want it to set yet. Decorate the top of the cheesecake with the strawberry halves and pour over the cooled jelly mixture. Return it to the refrigerator for another hour, until set.

VARIATIONS Try using lemon and lime jelly with a citrus-flavoured yogurt, or raspberry-flavoured jelly and yogurt.

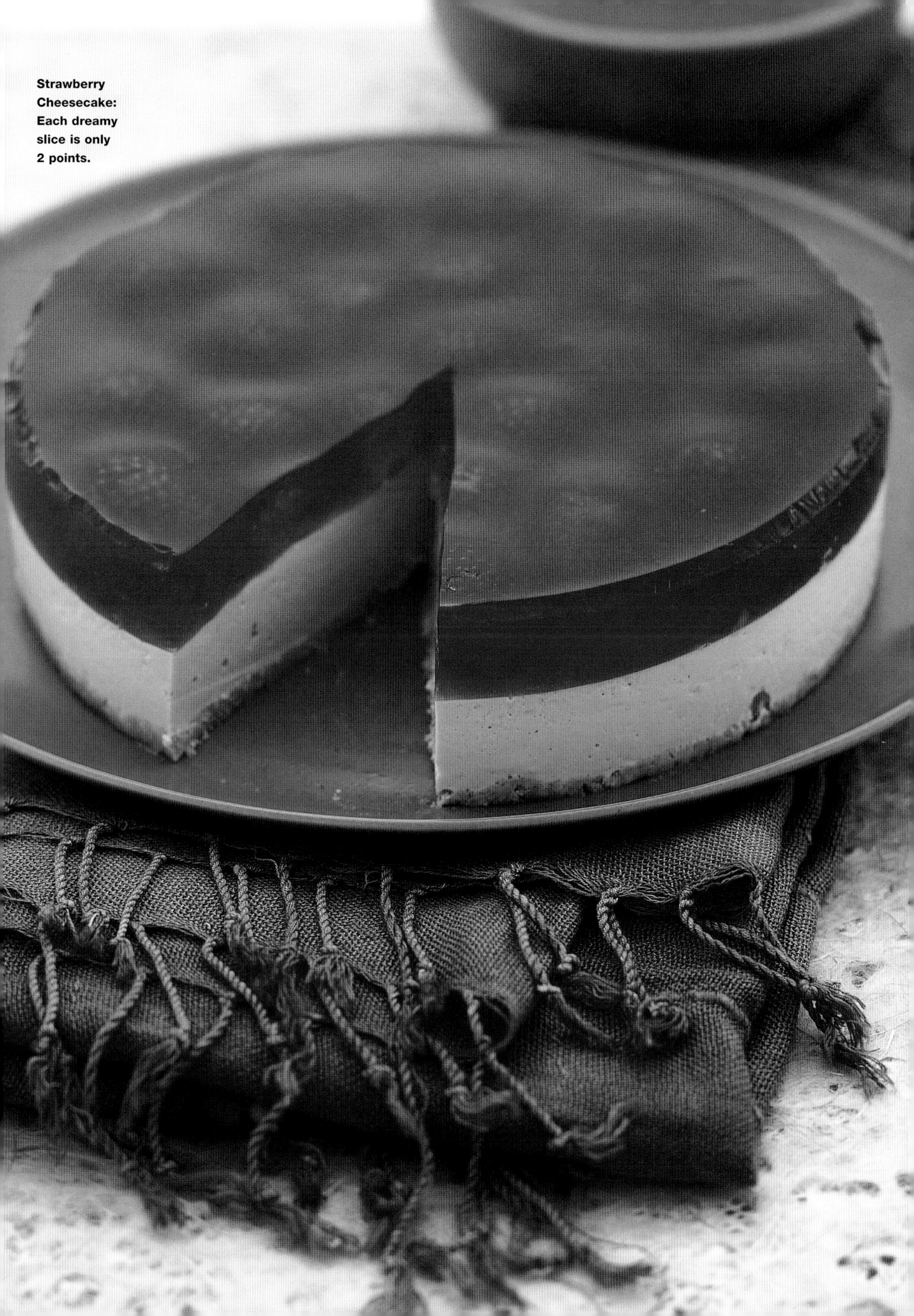

Strawberry Cheesecake: Each dreamy slice is only 2 points.

cakes
bakes & biscuits

This chapter is full of wonderful recipes to satisfy you. The beauty of the Weight Watchers diet is that you never have to deprive yourself of the foods you love. Thanks to the hard work, imagination and cooking skills of our contestants, here is a whole chapter of cakes, bakes and biscuits that you can eat without gaining weight. Most can be frozen too, so you can avoid temptation – eat one portion and put the rest away for another day, or for when friends drop in.

PINEAPPLE AND PASSION-FRUIT SQUARES

POINTS

per recipe: 22½   per serving: 2

V *if using free-range eggs*
Makes 12 squares
Preparation time: 15 minutes
Cooking time: 25–30 minutes
Calories per serving: 125
Freezing: recommended

Mrs Maureen Waldron is a Gold Member from Smethwick in the West Midlands. She loves the Weight Watchers cookbooks for their baking recipes, as she and her husband both have a sweet tooth which they like to indulge without putting on weight. This recipe was developed for her husband who loves the moist texture of brownies, but isn't a fan of chocolate. It has been tried and tested on the family to great approval, especially when served with ice cream.

175 g (6 oz) caster sugar

1 medium egg

2 egg whites

4 canned unsweetened pineapple rings, drained and puréed in a food processor

1 tablespoon sunflower oil

25 ml (¾ fl oz) passion-fruit juice, made from the sieved pulp of 1 large passion-fruit

125 g (4½ oz) self-raising white flour

a pinch of salt

15 g (½ oz) flaked almonds

1 Preheat the oven to Gas Mark 4/ 180°C/fan oven 160°C. Line a 20 cm × 20 cm (8-inch × 8-inch) baking tin with non-stick baking parchment.

2 In a large bowl beat together the sugar, whole egg and egg whites, puréed pineapple, oil and passion-fruit juice. Fold in the flour and salt.

3 Pour the mixture into the prepared tin and sprinkle over the almonds. Bake in the oven for 25–30 minutes until risen and golden, and a skewer inserted in the middle comes out clean.

4 Leave to cool before removing from the tin. Cut into 12 portions.

TOP TIP Keep in an airtight container for up to three days.

VARIATION Try using four peach halves instead of pineapple.

Pineapple and Passion-Fruit Squares: A satisfying treat with tea or coffee.

CHEESE AND HERB SCONES

POINTS

per recipe: 26½   per serving: 1½

Ⓥ *if using a free-range egg and vegetarian cheese*

Makes 18 scones

Preparation time: 20 minutes

Cooking time: 10–15 minutes

Calories per scone: 90

Freezing: recommended

Mrs Mollie Gath from Selby in North Yorkshire has been a Member of Weight Watchers for several years. She has four children and three grandchildren with another on the way, and loves reading, patchwork, line and tap-dancing. She loves scones spread with cottage cheese or a zero-point topping such as sliced tomato and cucumber.

Cheese and Herb Scones: Only 1½ points for a whole scone.

---

250 g (9 oz) self-raising white flour

1 teaspoon mustard powder

¼ teaspoon baking powder

a pinch of salt

50 g (1¾ oz) polyunsaturated margarine

1½ teaspoons mixed dried herbs

75 g (2¾ oz) half-fat Cheddar cheese, grated

1 medium egg

50 ml (2 fl oz) low-fat plain yogurt

50 ml (2 fl oz) skimmed milk

---

1 Preheat the oven to Gas Mark 7/ 220°C/fan oven 200°C and line a baking tray with non-stick baking parchment.

2 In a mixing bowl, sieve together the flour, mustard powder, baking powder and salt. Rub in the margarine until the mixture resembles coarse breadcrumbs. Stir in the herbs and cheese.

3 In a measuring jug beat together the egg and yogurt, and then make up the quantity to 150 ml (¼ pint) with skimmed milk. Add this to the other ingredients, stirring together with a palette knife.

4 Draw together the mixture with your fingertips to make a soft dough, and turn out on to a floured work surface. Roll out gently to 5 mm (¼-inch) thick and use a small cutter – 4 cm (1½ inches) in diameter – to cut out the scones. Roll out any leftover dough to make more scones.

5 Place the scones on the prepared baking tray. Bake for 10–15 minutes until risen and golden. Cool on a rack or eat them warm.

TOP TIP Handle the dough mixture as little as possible or else the scones may be tough.

TEA LOAF CAKE

POINTS

per recipe: 25½   per serving: 2

Ⓥ *if using a free-range egg*

Makes 12 slices

Preparation time: overnight soaking + 15 minutes

Cooking time: 45–50 minutes

Calories per slice: 140

Freezing: not recommended

Jenny McIntee is a Member from Colchester in Essex with two young sons. Within two weeks of joining Weight Watchers, she lost 6½ pounds. This recipe is an adaptation of one her mum used to make and is very quick and easy.

---

100 g (3½ oz) glacé cherries, halved

150 g (5½ oz) mixed fruit (any combination of raisins or sultanas)

75 g (2¾ oz) dark brown molasses sugar

225 ml (8 fl oz) strong black tea, cooled slightly

1 medium egg

100 g (3½ oz) plain self-raising flour

100 g (3½ oz) wholemeal self-raising flour

---

1 The evening before you want to make the cake, place the cherries, dried fruit and sugar in a large bowl and pour over the tea. Cover and leave to soak overnight in a cool place.

2 Preheat the oven to Gas Mark 3/ 160°C/fan oven 140°C and line a 450 g (1 lb) loaf tin with non-stick baking parchment.

3 Stir the egg and both flours into the fruit mixture and then spoon the whole lot into the prepared tin. Bake for 45–50 minutes, until firm to the touch and a skewer inserted into the middle comes out clean.

BERMUDA BANANA CAKE

POINTS

per recipe: 53½   per serving: 6

Ⓥ *if using a free-range egg*
Makes 9 slices
Preparation time: 15 minutes
Cooking time: 35–45 minutes
Calories per slice: 360
Freezing: recommended

Lun Alter is a Gold Member from Clydach in Swansea who joined Weight Watchers in January 1996 and reached her Goldstar Goal within eight months. But the weight crept back on and she rejoined in May. With the support of her Leaders, Anita and Lisa, she hopes to meet her new Goal soon.

5 very ripe small bananas
100 g (3½ oz) caster sugar
175 g (6 oz) polyunsaturated margarine
3 medium eggs
2 teaspoons vanilla essence
1 tablespoon whisky (optional)
250 g (9 oz) self-raising white flour
1 teaspoon baking powder

1 Preheat the oven to Gas Mark 4/ 180°C/fan oven 160°C and line a 450 g (1 lb) loaf tin with non-stick baking parchment.
2 Mash the bananas in a large bowl and then add the sugar, margarine, eggs, vanilla and whisky, if using, and beat together well with a hand or electric whisk.
3 In a separate bowl, sieve together the flour and baking powder, and then add to the banana mixture. Whisk again until well mixed.
4 Immediately tip into the prepared loaf tin. Bake for 35–40 minutes, until risen and firm to the touch.

BANANA GINGERBREAD SLICES

POINTS

per recipe: 41   per serving: 2

Ⓥ *if using free-range eggs*
Makes 20 slices
Preparation time: 15 minutes + cooling
Cooking time: 35–40 minutes
Calories per slice: 140
Freezing: recommended

Mrs Rosalind Leatherbarrow is a Gold Member from Acocks Green in Birmingham. She joined Weight Watchers in March 1994 and reached her Goal weight within 10 months and has kept the weight off ever since. She has been married for 30 years to John and they have two married sons, Carl and Anthony, and a three year-old grandson. She works part-time at a bank and loves cooking, especially for her sweet tooth, hence the gingerbread made with her favourites, bananas and sultanas.

275 g (9½ oz) plain white flour
1 teaspoon bicarbonate of soda
4 teaspoons ground ginger
2 teaspoons mixed spice
100 g (3½ oz) soft light-brown sugar
4 tablespoons sunflower oil
2 tablespoons black treacle
2 tablespoons malt extract
2 medium eggs
4 tablespoons orange juice
3 small bananas, mashed
100 g (3½ oz) sultanas

1 Preheat the oven to Gas Mark 4/ 180°C/fan oven 160°C. Line an approximately 28 cm × 18 cm (11-inch × 7-inch) baking tin with non-stick baking parchment.
2 Reserve a tablespoon of flour and sift the rest with the bicarbonate of soda, ginger and mixed spice into a bowl. Sift the sugar with the reserved tablespoon of flour, and then stir this into the flour and ginger mixture.
3 Make a well in the centre of the flour mix, and add the oil, treacle, malt extract, eggs, orange juice, bananas and sultanas. Mix well.
4 Turn the mixture into the prepared tin and bake in the oven for 35–40 minutes, or until a skewer inserted into the middle comes out clean.
5 Leave to cool in the tin for 5 minutes, and then turn out on to a wire rack to cool completely. Cut into 20 slices to serve.

VARIATIONS Try vanilla rather than ginger, and dried mixed peel instead of sultanas.

Banana Gingerbread Slices: Absolutely fantastic.

Apple and Sultana Muffins: Marvellous muffins for only 1½ points each.

APPLE AND SULTANA MUFFINS

POINTS

per recipe: 32½	per muffin: 1½

Ⓥ *if using a free-range egg*

Makes 24 muffins
Preparation time: 15 minutes
Cooking time: 15 minutes
Calories per muffin: 85
Freezing: recommended

Darren Wellock from Irlam in Manchester used his previous catering experience to develop this recipe. He has lost 16 pounds in the eight weeks since he joined and still enjoys his cakes immensely.

75 g (2¾ oz) polyunsaturated margarine
100 g (3½ oz) caster sugar
1 medium egg, beaten
2 teaspoons vanilla essence
180 g jar of apple sauce
1 large dessert apple, peeled and diced
50 g (1¾ oz) sultanas
200 g (7 oz) self-raising white flour
1 teaspoon baking powder
1 teaspoon ground cinnamon

1 Preheat the oven to Gas Mark 5/ 190°C/fan oven 170°C. Place 24 cake cases in two muffin trays.
2 Cream the margarine and sugar in a large mixing bowl, and then add the egg and vanilla essence – mix well. Finally add the apple sauce, apple and sultanas, and stir together.
3 Sift the flour, baking powder and cinnamon into another bowl.
4 Add the dry ingredients to the wet and stir together – it's important to do this quickly if the muffins are to rise. Using a dessertspoon, quickly dollop the mixture into each of the cake cases, and then immediately place the muffins in the oven.
5 Bake for 12–15 minutes, until the muffins are risen, firm to the touch and golden-brown. Turn the muffins out of the tin but leave them in the cake cases on a wire rack until cool.

TOP TIP These muffins will keep in an airtight container for up to three days.

SCOTTISH SHORTBREAD

POINTS

per recipe: 54	per serving: 2½

Ⓥ Ⓥⓖ *Makes 24 biscuits*
Preparation time: 15 minutes
Cooking time: 15 minutes
Calories per biscuit: 130
Freezing: not recommended

Mrs Mary Henderson is a Member from Hornchurch in Essex. She is 71 years old and partially disabled, so she finds exercise impossible and has to rely on diet alone to stay slim. She enjoys the Weight Watchers Meetings with her Leader, Barbara's, genuine interest in each Member making all the difference. This recipe has been handed down through her family since her Grandmother's day.

225 g (8 oz) polyunsaturated margarine
125 g (4½ oz) caster sugar
50 g (1¾ oz) ground rice
225 g (8 oz) plain white flour
a pinch of salt
1 teaspoon caster sugar, for sprinkling

1 Preheat the oven to Gas Mark 4/ 180°C/fan oven 160°C and line a baking sheet with non-stick baking parchment.
2 Place the margarine, sugar and ground rice on a board and, with fingertips, draw them together until thoroughly mixed.
3 Add the flour by sprinkling it over in four batches and incorporating it each time with your fingertips but avoid over-working the mixture.
4 Roll or pat out the mixture to 5 mm (¼-inch) thickness, and then cut into rounds with a 5 cm (2-inch) cutter. Place the rounds on the prepared baking sheet and bake for 15 minutes, until golden brown. Sprinkle 1 teaspoon of caster sugar over all the shortbread and then cool on a wire rack.

TOP TIP It helps to keep the mixture cool or else it may become too sticky. The mixture can be refrigerated for 10 minutes or so before rolling out if it is too difficult.

Scottish Shortbread: Tastes just like the real thing.

HONEY AND LEMON SLICES

Ⓥ if using free-range eggs

Makes 16 slices

Preparation time: 10 minutes
+ 30 minutes cooling

Cooking time: 20–25 minutes

Calories per slice: 100

Freezing: recommended

Hayley Roberts is a Leader from
Pontefract in West Yorkshire. These
Honey and Lemon Slices satisfy her
cravings – eaten on their own or with
a lemon yogurt.

2 medium eggs
2 medium egg whites
175 g (6 oz) caster sugar
2 tablespoons lemon juice
2 tablespoons lemon curd
2 tablespoons sunflower oil
1 tablespoon clear honey
100 g (3½ oz) self-raising white flour

1 Preheat the oven to Gas Mark 3/
160°C/fan oven 140°C and line a
Swiss roll tin with non-stick baking
parchment.
2 Whisk the eggs and egg whites
together with the sugar, lemon juice,
lemon curd, sunflower oil and
honey, preferably using an electric
whisk. Whisk for about 3 minutes,
until very light and fluffy.
3 Gently fold in the flour. Pour the
mixture into the tin. Bake for 20–25
minutes, until a skewer inserted in
the middle comes out clean.
4 Leave to cool for 30 minutes before
taking it out of the tin. Remove the
baking paper and cut into 16 slices.

VARIATION Try orange rather than
lemon juice.

DIETERS' DELIGHT

Ⓥ if using free-range eggs

Makes 12 slices

Preparation time: 20 minutes + cooling

Cooking time: 1 hour 10 minutes

Calories per slice: 170

Freezing: recommended

Mrs Winnie Young is a Member from
Swinton in Manchester. She has lost
8½ pounds in 11 weeks and is now
satisfied with herself. To stay that
way and eat her favourite home-
baked pies and cakes she came up
with this recipe.

25 g (1 oz) polyunsaturated margarine
50 g (1¾ oz) caster sugar
4 medium eggs
175 g (6 oz) self-raising white flour
1 teaspoon baking powder
1 medium carrot, grated
100 g (3½ oz) moist, ready-to-eat apricots, chopped
100 g (3½ oz) raisins
100 g (3½ oz) sultanas

1 Preheat the oven to Gas Mark 2/
150°C/fan oven 130°C and line a
450 g (1 lb) loaf tin with non-stick
baking parchment.
2 Cream together the margarine and
sugar until pale. Add the eggs and
then the flour and baking powder.
Finally fold in the carrot, apricots,
raisins and sultanas. Alternatively you
could mix the whole lot together in a
food processor.
3 Spoon the mixture into the prepared
tin. Bake in the oven for 1 hour
10 minutes until risen and golden,
and a skewer inserted in the middle
comes out clean. Turn out on a wire
rack and allow to cool. Cut into
12 slices.

BLUEBERRY AND APPLE CAKE

Ⓥ if using free-range eggs

Serves 10

Preparation time: 30 minutes

Cooking time : 45–50 minutes

Calories per slice: 125

Freezing: not recommended

Jill Parsons is a Member from
Brentwood in Essex with two
teenagers. She created this cake
as a treat for herself while dieting
but it's also for her husband who
is a diabetic, hence no sugar.

150 g (5½ oz) self-raising white flour
2 teaspoons baking powder
25 g (1 oz) polyunsaturated margarine
50 g (1¾ oz) ground almonds
2 medium eggs
grated zest and juice of 1 orange
½ teaspoon almond essence
2 medium dessert apples, peeled, cored and diced
125 g (4½ oz) blueberries

1 Preheat the oven to Gas Mark 6/
200°C/fan oven 180°C and line a
20 cm (8-inch) square tin with non-
stick baking parchment.
2 Place the flour, baking powder,
margarine, almonds, eggs, orange
zest and juice, and almond essence
together in a bowl. Beat thoroughly
by hand or with an electric whisk.
3 Fold in the apples and blueberries
and immediately spoon the mixture
into the prepared tin. Bake for
45–50 minutes, until firm to the
touch and a skewer inserted into the
middle comes out clean.
4 Leave to cool in the tin. Keep in
an airtight container for up to a week.

CHOCOLATE YOGURT CAKE

POINTS

per recipe: $39\frac{1}{2}$	per serving: $3\frac{1}{2}$

Ⓥ *if using free-range eggs*
Makes 12 slices
Preparation time: 15 minutes + cooling
Cooking time: 1 hour
Calories per slice: 205
Freezing: recommended

Louise Shilleto joined Weight Watchers with her sister in January 2001. She runs a coffee shop in Barnsley, South Yorkshire, her home town, and bakes frequently for the shop. She discovered this recipe by accident while trying to make a cake using her favourite chocolate-flavoured Mullerlite yogurt. Serve as an after-dinner treat with low-fat custard, adding the extra points.

225 g (8 oz) self-raising white flour

175 g (6 oz) caster sugar

100 g ($3\frac{1}{2}$ oz) polyunsaturated margarine

2 medium eggs

a few drops of vanilla essence

$\frac{1}{2}$ teaspoon baking powder

1 × 200 g pot Mullerlite chocolate yogurt

1 Preheat the oven to Gas Mark 4/ 180°C/fan oven 160°C. Grease and line a 25 cm × 20 cm (10-inch × 8-inch) oblong baking tin with non-stick baking parchment.
2 Put all the ingredients in a mixing bowl and, using an electric hand beater on full speed, mix to a smooth batter.
3 Pour the mixture into the baking tin and bake in the oven for 50–60 minutes, until firm to the touch and a skewer inserted into the middle comes out clean. Turn out on to a

Chocolate Yogurt Cake: Cake and custard heaven!

wire rack and allow to cool. Cut into 12 slices.

TOP TIP Wrap the cake slices individually and place in the freezer. They can be taken out when needed for packed lunches or picnics.

VARIATIONS Try this with other flavours of Mullerlite, such as toffee. You could also use a lemon and lime yogurt with the zests of a lemon and lime in the batter too.